Talk
To Me

Talk To Me

MUNROE BERGDORF

PENGUIN BOOKS

PENGUIN BOOKS

UK | USA | Canada | Ireland | Australia
India | New Zealand | South Africa

Penguin Books is part of the Penguin Random House group of companies
whose addresses can be found at global.penguinrandomhouse.com.

www.penguin.co.uk
www.puffin.co.uk
www.ladybird.co.uk

Penguin
Random House
UK

First published 2025

001

Text copyright © Munroe Bergdorf, 2025

The moral right of the author has been asserted

Set in 10/16pt Sabon LT Pro
Typeset by Jouve (UK), Milton Keynes
Printed and bound in Great Britain by Clays Ltd, Elcograf S.p.A.

The authorized representative in the EEA is Penguin Random House Ireland,
Morrison Chambers, 32 Nassau Street, Dublin D02 YH68

A CIP catalogue record for this book is available from the British Library

ISBN: 978-0-241-66292-2

All correspondence to:
Penguin Books
Penguin Random House Children's
One Embassy Gardens, 8 Viaduct Gardens, London SW11 7BW

Talk To Me is dedicated to all the brave young voices across the world. Stand tall together in solidarity and keep existing loudly. A better world is possible for us all.

'You cannot, you cannot use someone else's fire.
You can only use your own. And in order to do that,
you must first be willing to believe that you have it.'
– Audre Lorde

CONTENTS

Introduction

It all begins with a conversation. Conversations are the start – they're how we can change *everything*.

I know how much you have to say. How powerful your words are. There are so many thoughts and questions circling your mind and today, *now*, is the time to set them out into the world.

We're living through such an exciting time in history.

In many ways, we're living in an era of enlightenment.

Think about how many people you have access to connect with every single day; how many stories you can hear; and how many different perspectives you are exposed to. That might come through books, thanks to more diverse voices being published, or via the internet – your social media feed is full of people telling you about their experiences. They're talking about what it feels like to live inside their bodies; how their brains might differ from yours; or what it's like to live where they do – whether that's in a war zone, in a different culture, or under a different government to yours, you can hear from their mouths, *in real time*, what that's like. We now have access to hear from those who were once kept silent.

There was once a time when we only heard from those who traditional media and broadcast companies deemed worthy of being listened to, and people from minority groups struggled to be heard. To be completely honest with you, that still happens. But more and more, we are seeing others come forward, creating their own avenues to tell their stories.

And you can do the same.

We're living on the same Earth as all these wonderful activists – fellow human beings doing incredible things, and we can learn from them. We're seeing vital points of discussion being raised and we're able to question those in power, challenge them and ask them why things are the way they are. So many of us, myself included, have begun to ask these questions and explore what we can do to change the world that we live in. Resistance movements are being formed. And they're also being *noticed*.

The sad thing is a lot of what we are talking about isn't new. We've always been here; it's just that now we can reach more people with our message and pull more people into our cause, or encourage them to campaign for their own causes and find the things that they care about.

How can we do that? By coming together and using the power that we have – our voices – to make them listen. Whether that's by taking to the streets in protest, giving voice to our experiences on social media or simply starting important conversations at home with our families, our words are our power.

When we fight for what's right, we might face push-back from those who want everything to remain exactly as it is.

As more of us take to the streets in protest, governments across the world begin stripping back our rights to do so. As more of us discuss our true gender identities, we face challenges from those who deny us the things we need to feel fully confident in our bodies.

I'll be exploring examples of this throughout the book, but what I'm beginning to recognize is that this push-back is nothing new. It's a pattern that has happened before and will happen again.

It's daunting, I know. I used to think that there was no way that I could make a difference; I felt silenced by my environment and everyone around me. I felt like I didn't have a voice.

But I *did* – and as soon as I found it and nurtured it, things began to change. Not just for me, and how I felt about myself and my own life, but also in the world around me. I noticed that by speaking out, I was helping to open people's minds. They could see my reality and begin to understand it better.

I want you to learn, much like I did, that you *can* do something about the injustices you see in this world. Stick with me, and I'll show you how you can engage in true, valuable communication – the type that brings about change. Throughout this book, I will be sharing some of the most valuable lessons I've learned throughout my life so far. I'm going to be telling you about how I went from being a lost teenager in a small town to where I am today – a person who is confident in the knowledge that not only do I have a voice, but that my voice *makes a real difference.*

With this knowledge I've been able to carve out a career that encompasses modelling, presenting, writing, advocacy and activism. I've been awarded an honorary doctorate for my work campaigning for transgender rights, by the University of Brighton, and I was appointed as a National Advocate for UN Women UK. I'm an ambassador for gender-variant and transgender youth charity Mermaids, which makes me so incredibly proud as I can see the difference I'm making within my own community. There are not many trans people in the UK who have large platforms, so I feel especially passionate about using mine to try to positively influence people in the best way that I know how – by having big and important conversations and by striving to be the change I want to see.

A good conversation, to me, is a meeting of minds. It's discussing and listening to each other's perspectives on a matter in a safe space, where each person is truly holding space for and hearing the other. And we need to talk about how to have these conversations to jump-start your activism.

Activism: The action of campaigning to bring about political or social change.

Activism is active, not passive.

What I mean by this is that activism *isn't* . . .

- silent. It doesn't come from crossing your arms and thinking, '*I can't make a difference.*'
- idle. It also doesn't come from sitting back and saying, however loudly, 'This is wrong,' over and over again without doing anything about it.

Activism *is* about . . .

- bringing people together.
- doing small things that make a big difference.
- working as a collective.
- using what you already have.
- learning about yourself.

But how do you do that?

In Part 1 we'll be finding out who you are . . . and what lights you up!

I was 24 years old when I began my medical transition. This journey allowed the truth of who I was to come to the surface. It allowed what has always been there – and what society had told me not to be – to shine through. At the time I was living in East London and meeting other people in the queer community, learning, listening and reading about other trans people's experiences and lives. I was having conversations that were new to me and, through sharing my story and listening to others, I had my eyes opened. It helped me find my power, my confidence and my voice, and to strip myself of my own shame so that I could express myself in a fuller and more authentic way, and become someone I was truly proud of.

This began my journey of other self-discoveries – not just to do with who I was and my own personal experience, but also how all of the injustice in the world is connected. And with this, I began to understand how to use my experiences and voice to bring about real change.

This is what we'll be discussing in the first part of the book: how to examine who you are, what fires you up and where your passions could be best used. I'll help you identify who your community are, and how to feel confident sharing your thoughts and opinions with them.

We'll also talk about one of the most valuable skills you have: listening. Our world is full of fascinating people – even those that we may disagree with. There's so much to be learned from people whose views don't align with our own and sometimes this can lead to the most important conversations of all.

In Part 2 we'll be learning how – and when – to speak up.

In my early years and my teens, I struggled to connect the dots. I had a lot of questions that I didn't have the answers to. I could see injustice, but it felt like everyone wanted to keep everything *exactly* as it was, instead of finding ways that the world, and the people in it, could change.

I grew up in the 1990s in the small, sleepy town of Stansted Mountfitchet on the Hertfordshire–Essex border in England. It was picturesque – we were surrounded by rolling countryside and all the houses had perfectly tended-to lawns. It was traditional, quaint and sweet. Ideal for anyone else . . . but not for me. This was the 1990s, and Section 28 (the law that banned the promotion of homosexuality in schools) was in full force. Books that showed queer lifestyles were banned, and teachers – even if they wanted to, or were in one themselves – weren't allowed to speak to their students about same-sex relationships. If they did, they faced disciplinary action. LGBTQIA+ students and faculty alike were pushed into silence.

We were a mixed-race family – my mum is white, British and my dad is Black, Jamaican – and, in my small town, there weren't many other mixed-race or Black families. I had a happy childhood but as I grew into a teenager, I couldn't see myself reflected anywhere. I didn't see anyone else like me, hear their stories or see them lead fulfilled, successful lives.

I felt entirely censored by society and by those around me. I lived in a constant state of hypervigilant self-surveillance where I wasn't letting myself truly *be* myself: I was afraid to walk how I would naturally walk; I was afraid to speak in the tone that came naturally to me; I was afraid to tell people my true interests and hobbies; I was afraid to say how I was truly feeling, who I was attracted to and my opinions on important subjects. But as unfair and alienating as that was for me, it seemed that everyone around me was just happy to accept things the way they were.

I felt alone, confused and frustrated.

Then I arrived at university, and my life changed. By leaving behind my small town, I expanded my world. Suddenly I was in Brighton, surrounded by people who were challenging the world around them, and I started having all these incredible conversations. I was having discussions with my peers, speaking about why things were the way they were – why did we assume people were straight, unless they told us otherwise? Why did we demand that people must come out just because they were queer, when we didn't demand the same for straight people? Why did society try to make us hide who we were? Who did it benefit? Was there an alternative way that society could be?

That process of being able to speak out loud and have these conversations really helped me to understand *why* I felt so confused and so frustrated. And, once I started talking, I found I couldn't stop. I began to grow my platform and speak to wider audiences.

I had incredibly tricky conversations where people challenged me on my views and my identity. I got things wrong sometimes. I learned some tough lessons as I knew speaking up was so valuable, but at times, it left me drained. And I'd realize nothing had changed. So while I want to show you how to speak up when you feel you need to, I also want to help you identify when it's just not worth it.

In Part 3 we'll be opening up the discussion.

There's this phrase: 'We're living in unprecedented times.' It's said almost every time there's a major news story dominating the front pages and our feeds. It implies

8

that we are living through a rollercoaster of hardship that's worse, and more unusual, than anything the people before us may have gone through.

I don't think this is necessarily true – we have always lived in unprecedented times. What is largely unprecedented is our ability to access what's really going on in the world, and how we can view these huge world events. We are able to listen to a huge diversity of perspectives and we carry that ability with us in our pockets. The information, situations and events that we are now seeing have always been there; it's just that we're not used to being exposed to it all 24 hours a day.

We're also more divided than ever before. For example, research shows that in the UK young women are becoming more progressive and open-minded on issues such as feminism and race, as opposed to young men. In the US, three in ten young men believe that in 20 years it will be more difficult to be a man than a woman, while young women believe the opposite.[1] In the US, the two major political parties – the Democrats and the Republicans – have vastly different views on issues like abortion, with the Republicans rolling back abortion rights (at the time of writing, abortion has now been banned in a dozen states). Transgender people are facing a threat to their rights, with debates over what public spaces we should be 'allowed' to access and gender-affirming care also being banned in twenty-six states at the time of writing.

It's hard to know where to seek out the answers to complex questions. We can either find ourselves stuck listening only to those who have views similar to us, or in an argument where we're drowning each other out rather than listening.

That's why, in the final part of the book, we're going to be taking everything we've discussed so far and putting it into practice. We're going to talk about a wide range of important issues, and I want to equip you with the confidence to go out and have all these world-expanding conversations with those around you.

Change starts with dialogue. By gathering information, creating community, talking to each other . . . and *actually listening*. This is what helps us to cut through the noise and say what needs to be said.

And there's no greater act of defiance than using your voice.

Part 1

—

The Beginning of Your Journey

—

Writing this book has felt heavy at times. I've struggled with having to reflect on so many issues that feel very close to home. It's been tempting to shut my laptop, curl up on the sofa and cuddle my pets. But I don't want to feel hopeless, and I certainly don't want you to feel hopeless. And while I don't have all the answers to solve everything that's happening in the world, I do know that change is possible.

Change can be both big and small. It can be at a community or systemic level, or even just within your family or friendship group. Having conversations with the people around you and viewing the world through a different lens is how we expand our own minds and inspire others to do the same. And no conversation is too small.

So where do you start? How do you find the cause that lights you up and excites you? You're setting off on a journey of self-discovery, and that starts with digging deep into who you are and what you're passionate about.

1

We Need to Talk About . . . You

Some of the most important conversations you'll *ever* have are the ones you're going to have with yourself.

This can mean asking yourself tough questions, like, *'Why does this make me feel uncomfortable?'* and *'Are the people I surround myself with bringing out my best side?'* It won't always feel great and will open some hard truths. Change can feel scary. But it's a part of life. None of us can grow without it. You, like me, are a human who is ever evolving. We're going to need to ask ourselves these tough questions to find the cause that lights us up.

There is a lot of injustice in the world, which can make it hard to know what to fight for. Perhaps you already know which cause is closest to your heart, but don't worry if you don't. You may look around you and feel that everyone apart from you seems to know what they're doing. But I promise that's not true. It can take time to find the thing that fires you up, and it's important to remember it's not a race.

What lights you up?

The world can feel very loud at times. Whether it's looking at the news headlines of the day, or opening up your social media feeds, there is so much that demands our attention and that we need to talk about in order to bring about change.

In reality, you can't fight every injustice there is. There was a time when I tried, and all it led to was me feeling exhausted, burned out and bitter. It's a hard pill to swallow, but it was only when I pulled back and began to think more about who I am and what I truly care about that I was able to find focus and home in on my activism and cause.

When I speak about finding your cause, what I really mean is finding the thing that makes you feel like you have purpose and that makes you want to jump out of bed each morning.

For me, my cause has always been opening the conversation surrounding trans rights. I want to show the world our humanity and fight against the decisions made by those in power that impact our daily lives. It's not the *only* thing I speak out on, but I've found it's best to focus in on one or two things that you can really devote your time and energy to.

That's why, at first, I want you to dig deep into yourself and figure out what truly lights you up. That's where I began:

I thought about my life and my experiences, and I started to think about what the most effective way would be for me to bring about change. This was in 2015, and at the time there weren't many trans people talking openly about their lives, and I knew that was where I wanted to lend my voice.

I can now look at myself and feel proud of who I am and what I've achieved. But I didn't reach this place overnight. I've had to do a lot of intense self-work, frequently challenging myself in how I think. I suffer from anxiety, and when I have anxiety attacks it feels like there are no words to describe it. I feel an overwhelming sense of impending doom. But when I self-soothe and feel calmer, I can usually figure out where that doom is rooted or what triggered it by asking myself questions. Then I can begin to find my way out of it.

And it's the same with finding the cause that you care about the most, finding your *why*.

You could begin by looking around you and thinking about the moments that spark deep emotions within you.

Ask yourself:

- When was the last time I felt angry at something I felt was unjust, unfair or wrong?
- What was it about that situation that made me feel that way?
- Who does this situation impact?

You might ponder these questions yourself as you go about your day-to-day life, or you might want to journal or record yourself a voice memo. Or you could get together with friends and discuss the world around you. Do whatever makes you feel comfortable.

Your anger could have been sparked by something that happened in your school, university or workplace. Is someone being made to feel unwelcome? For example, you may have noticed that certain areas are not wheelchair accessible, or perhaps there's a culture of bullying that isn't being taken seriously.

Or your anger might have been sparked by something you've seen on the news or on social media. Has something happened that made you feel ashamed of the world you live in? Are decisions being made by those in power that you don't agree with? For example, has a law been passed that is going to negatively impact you or other people?

When I see or hear the news and I feel my heart begin to race at an emerging story, I take time to figure out what it is about the story that is making me feel that way. Often there's anger and sometimes sadness too. By pinpointing *how* the story is making me feel, I can then begin to figure out *why* it is making me feel that way. Is it because I know the impact this story will have on my friends, and my family?

Or is it because I just know, in my bones, that people are being treated unfairly? You may come across stories happening on a more global scale that have no direct impact on you, your friends or your family, but which you can still recognize are wrong. We don't have to just look for issues that surround us or directly impact our lives. Every single human right is linked and only focusing on the issues that affect you directly can make you neglect the wider issues. Something that feels like it's happening 'over there' might also impact you 'here' more than you realize. You will have more power to change it than you think.

For example, there may be a war happening in another country, and because it's happening far away, you might not think it's something to pay attention to or care about. But our government, or even the companies we give our money to, may be funding that war. They may be directly contributing to the suffering of others.

Similarly with climate change, we may not (yet) be directly seeing its impact where we live, but extreme weather is causing death and poverty around the world. Our actions and lifestyle choices – from the clothes we buy to the way we travel – can have a huge impact on the planet.

Once you've begun to pinpoint the causes that make you feel fired up, you could then ask yourself the following:

● Why is this happening?
● Who else might also be upset by this situation?
● What would need to change for me to feel differently about it?

Don't worry too much if at this stage the solution feels too big or impossible for you to do alone. Creating change is never just your responsibility.

Finding your role in the machine

You're asking yourself some big questions here, and it's very easy to feel overwhelmed. You might also be wondering if there's any point in you even trying. It can all seem too big. After all, a lot of the wider issues impacting the world are caused by decisions completely out of your control. Take climate change, for example – the richest 1 per cent of the global population account for more greenhouse gas emissions than the poorest 50 per cent.[2] Watching people in power make decisions that impact the lives of everyone else can be incredibly frustrating, and it can make you feel like you can't bring about change yourself. But you can. You hold so much power.

I came to recognize my own power by thinking of activism as a machine. There's so much going on inside most machines that we simply don't see: we know that the big cogs are the pieces that shudder the machine into action, but it's the smaller cogs that, by joining together, prompt the bigger cogs into motion. If we think of activism this way, it's clear that we are often only exposed to the big cogs – those whose work we can admire and see. Behind the scenes, these people (or cogs), are supported by others working together on a smaller and more local scale to create action. Everyone has a place in the activism machine, and no cog is more or less important than the other. It's just about finding which role you're going to play.

Like I said earlier, for a while, I felt like everything was my fight. I could see that humans were being denied their autonomy, their freedom and their rights. And as much as I wanted to help everyone, eventually I realized I couldn't take on every cause in equal measure – it's just not effective or sustainable. So I thought about what would be the most effective way for me to bring about change, and I began talking about what I know the most: my own personal experience.

I hadn't seen myself reflected *anywhere* at this point. There was hardly any media representation of trans people and it had, for so long, made me feel like I was the only person in the whole world who was questioning their gender identity. That caused me a lot of pain, and by piecing together what was causing me pain, I realized that by speaking out I could find my role in the machine. I could give a face to a group of people who had, historically, not been considered.

I would broadcast my thoughts out loud to anyone who would listen. I first started speaking up in 2015, when I was feeling this immense sense of frustration with the way the world was treating trans people. And once I started using my platform to talk about it, I refused to stop screaming about it.

Not everyone likes to share their thoughts so publicly though. You might prefer to have an open dialogue with friends about a particular issue or something you've seen in the news. Or maybe you like to post about it online. Or perhaps you prefer to speak with people who you know feel and experience similar things to you. No conversation is too small. Having these conversations opens your mind to other people's beliefs, feelings and perspectives. You can learn from their viewpoints and they can learn from yours, and this dialogue can get the machine's cogs moving in the right way.

You could even look to others who have brought about change and examine how they went about it and who helped them get there. I'm a big fan of the work Gina Martin has done. After having a horrible experience when a man took photos up her skirt at a music festival without her consent, she learned that there was no specific crime to charge him with. She set about to change that. At first, she used social media to ask if anyone had experienced anything similar to her, and gathered support and signatures for a petition. Then, working with a legal team (who gave her their expertise free of charge), she managed to have the law changed in 2019. Since then, she's been doing a large majority of her work offline, working in schools across Australia, discussing the impact of gender stereotypes on young people. Her work is so admirable as she, from her own personal experience, noticed a flaw in our systems and has since worked alongside others to bring about real change. It was her campaign, but she couldn't have achieved what she did without starting a conversation and bringing in other people's voices to her cause. She was part of a machine.

You may not be able to pinpoint your role in the machine right away – that will take some time as getting to know who you are, and what you want to stand for, is a lifelong process. This isn't just a checklist, or a chapter you can read to suddenly reach *there*.

We're always growing, we're always changing, but we are never alone.

Educating yourself

Information is – and always will be – our biggest asset. Have you ever found yourself in a conversation with someone where you know exactly what you believe in, but suddenly feel too intimidated to make your point? It's that feeling when deep down you know what you *want* to say, but you just don't have the right example, the right answers or all the information you need to make your point.

I have felt like this before, many times. And when this happens, I do the one thing I know can help – I absorb and learn as much as I can.

This, again, is a lifelong process. We'll never stop learning. I still have so much to learn, but I've found that by expanding my knowledge, digging deeper and reading more widely, I've been able to grow my confidence and find my voice.

As an activist, you do *have* to be confident, but this confidence can come in many forms. You don't have to be an extrovert or the loudest person in the room, but the confidence does have to exist on the inside. Whether you're having a one-on-one conversation with someone or giving a public speech about something you believe in, you will need that internal confidence to have conviction in what you're saying. People will see that you know yourself and your beliefs, and then they are more likely to listen. And this belief – this confidence – comes from knowing what you are talking about.

You don't need to be the one talking until you're ready.

My activism journey really began at university, when I was exposed to all of those new people and ideas that I hadn't encountered in my hometown. Back then, my queer community was mostly found in nightclubs and bars, as there weren't the same number of panel talks or debates being held as there are now. It was during parties and at night that I managed to get perspective on the experiences of other members of my community. I was seeing drag shows for the first time and meeting other trans people – all these bold, beautiful, colourful people who were being so defiant in who they were. Like me, they had grown up being told that gender was indisputable and that we had to live exactly as we were assigned at birth. But they were living their lives on their terms, showing the world that we *can* challenge gender norms, and that just because we're told to exist within the confines of the box we were born into, *we don't have to*. We can be whoever we want to be. I began to see the limitless breadth at which we could live.

I started going to talks. I'd sit in the back and just observe, soaking up as much as I could. I'd go to debates, panels and book events. Some of the more pivotal talks I attended were the ACAS (African, Caribbean and Asian society) meetings, which were held on a different university campus to my own that wasn't particularly diverse. I'd sneak in with friends and listen to people share their experiences. I realized how much my own knowledge of race had been shaped by the limited information supplied to me in school, and how I'd only been shown and taught history through a white-washed lens. It helped me to begin to challenge what I thought I knew, and to look deeper into myself as to how I'd been shaped by growing up mixed-race but only viewing the world through this one-sided viewpoint. I began to seek out more sources of information and read as widely as possible, before I felt ready to speak up.

If you believe in yourself, you won't be silenced.

Where to start

There are so many different and exciting ways to learn and gain a deeper understanding of the things that matter to you. You don't have to follow my path or go to university. You just need to find the method that suits you best. Here are some ideas for how you might seek out knowledge and grow your confidence:

- **Talk to people.** If you meet someone who has similar passions to you, listen and learn from them. You could also find out what art they like, what books they read, what events and festivals they go to, and see if any of these spark your interest.
- **Go to events.** There are so many panels, book events or groups and communities to join. You can find them online, in your local bookshop, or in a cafe or library by looking out for community noticeboards and seeing what upcoming events are advertised.
- **Look online.** From news websites to articles and interviews with people about their personal experience

on a matter, you can explore the facts and then hear directly about the experiences, opinions and beliefs of others.

- **Read.** There's no substitute for books, magazines and reputable newspapers. Read *everything* – both current literature *and* what's been published in the past. And always look beyond the most popular titles on one particular subject. If you read a feature in a magazine or newspaper, you could then use that as a jumping-off point to read further. What else has this person written? Whose work do they reference? Often online articles contain links in them that you can follow through and read. Or you could go to your local library and mention what particular writers you enjoy or time periods you want to read about, and a librarian could help you seek more information out.

But while I think it's important to read, discover and always be learning, you don't have to have all the answers. Yes, read as much as you can, but don't feel like you have to know *everything* in order to speak up and be heard. It's important to know enough that you feel confident in what you're saying, but a big part of that confidence is also knowing that it's impossible to have *all* the answers. You also need to be open to what comes next and what you'll learn as a result of a conversation. You will get things wrong (more on this in Chapter 4) but that's just another part of your journey and growth.

Take feminism – you don't have to know everything about feminism to be a feminist. To be a feminist all you really need to believe is that we all deserve equality, but you have to be willing to read up and learn from other people too. Then, as you look further into a topic, you might find there are views you simply don't relate to or agree with. Every movement has so many different viewpoints within it – whether that's feminism, the civil rights movement or the transgender movement. It's exciting to explore and understand these viewpoints, then find the ones that you relate to most.

The missing voices

It's vital that we can also recognize and identify what voices are missing from discussions. Often – particularly when reading historical texts – we are only being shown one point of view: that of those who were given a platform, which was often wealthy white men. Take what we learn in school – for me, my history lessons didn't discuss Black history from the perspective of the Black community. We were taught about racism and slavery, but the scale of suffering was minimized or removed, and the role our country's most powerful players had in upholding slavery was completely glossed over. I had to go out myself and learn about these topics from the perspective of the community who were living through it.

This was back in the 1990s, but there are still so many missing voices in what we're taught in school and also in the modern media. We are rarely shown the full picture. There aren't many working-class or diverse voices within journalism – this industry in particular is known for being tricky to enter if you aren't from a wealthy background, which means that when issues are covered, they are often reported on by people who don't have the relevant knowledge or lived experience. This could impact how they report on an issue. In other words, their personal bias can feed into their work, and they could end up writing in a way that tries to persuade you of their point of view without showing you the other side of the story.

For example, a writer from an upper-class background reporting on governmental issues may reap the benefits of a more right-wing party being in power, as their tax laws tend to benefit those who earn more. So, when they're writing about a right-wing government's decisions, they may do so in a more favourable way. This wouldn't matter as much if we were also hearing from working-class reporters, but as we now know, there are far fewer journalists with this background.

These sorts of biases could also impact the stories that are chosen to be relevant and reported on. For example, cases of white women who go missing often make headline news, while missing men, or women of colour, are often less reported on. This is another example of people in positions of power deciding which voices and communities matter.

So, read critically. Examine what an article or book is trying to tell you. Look at who the writer is, and think about who we aren't hearing from. It can sometimes be easy to read something and make the assumption that what you're reading is an accurate portrayal of what's happening now, or (if reading a historical text) what life was like at the time. But a critical reader will pull back and think about what isn't within that text and why it might not be there. They will then begin to seek out what's missing and find the other voices.

To think critically about what you're reading means . . .

- examining what the writer is trying to tell you and why they might be telling you that.
- thinking about their background and where their viewpoints are coming from.
- if they're of a certain demographic, asking yourself what another demographic might think of their opinion. If the writer is male, would women agree? If they're white, what might those of other ethnicities think of their opinions? Are they coming at this issue from a heteronormative viewpoint – as in, are they viewing the world only through their lens as a straight person?
- if it's a historical text, thinking about what else was going on at the time. Was there a particular viewpoint being presented as 'the norm', and who did this ignore? Who did it benefit?

When I first started reading feminist texts, Germaine Greer was one of the main voices of the time in the UK. She was a key figure in the second-wave feminism movement, which ran from the 1960s to 1980s and broadened the debate surrounding women's rights. Feminism had largely been focused on women gaining the vote and property rights, but during the second wave the movement also began to discuss how women are perceived in society, their sexuality and reproductive rights. The main voices of this wave of feminism tended to be – like Greer – middle-class and upper-class white women, and as a result ignored the experiences of women of colour and working-class women.

This meant some people would benefit from her teachings, but others would not. Upon realizing this, I began to seek out other voices: writers and activists like Maya Angelou, Dr Kimberlé Crenshaw, Toni Morrison and bell hooks, who all presented a fresh, inclusive perspective and looked at society as a whole.

Their work really helped me to join the dots on a huge number of different issues, from feminism to race. Their teachings were some of my first introductions to intersectional feminism and how everything is linked. The purpose of intersectional feminism is to recognize how different aspects of a person's identity might change the way they experience the world – and the barriers they might face as a result. I began to recognize how everything is linked. It isn't just about gender – it's about race; it's about class; it's about abilities; it's about sexuality. It's about all of the different intersecting components of someone's identity that may cause them to become marginalized within society.

My experiences as a Black trans woman and the ways in which I am perceived by others are entirely different from how a white cis woman encounters the world. I have to deal with racism and transphobia, on top of sexism. Intersectional feminism recognizes this, and by reading and expanding my knowledge in this area, I began to identify as a feminist and was able to have discussions with my peers about the individual barriers we faced within the world. But I was only able to get to this place by seeking out different work and alternative voices from those that were popular at the time in the world I was navigating.

You too can be active in your own education. Never just accept the first thing you come across. Dig deeper.

This is particularly important when you are finding out information via social media. It's such a big and fundamental part of our lives, but we must proceed with caution when using it as an educational tool . . .

Storytime – how Instagram changed the news

We hold so much information in our pockets and the palm of our hands. Our phones help us to instantly communicate with our friends, but also receive updates on news and what's happening around the world 24 hours a day, 7 days a week. Our phones are rarely out of our sight, and, as a result, social media is becoming our main source of news. 83 per cent of the UK's 16–24-year-olds consume news online, with our social media apps being the main driver to news websites, while 73 per cent consume news directly on social media.[3]

We also now follow people who are giving us updates on their lives in real time. This, I believe, is one of the good things about Instagram and TikTok – anyone with a phone can express their views and reach people on a global scale that would have been impossible before. We can listen and learn from those directly impacted by the issues we see in the news. For instance, people can now share, in real time, their experiences of life on the ground during a war, whereas previously they'd have had to have been found and interviewed by a war reporter who had been sent out there by a newspaper or news channel to share their information.

Then there are those who are opening up about their sexuality and gender identity, and using social media as a means to express all aspects of their lives – from their joy to their sadness. These are all people who would, if it wasn't for social media, have been voiceless, as they might not have had access to those working in the media or in publishing that they'd need to share their story. We can now see the intricacies and breadth of real people's lives. Being able to hear a variety of voices is one of the great things that social media has brought us.

So, who should you be following in order to ensure you're getting the widest possible perspective on a broad number of issues? I don't want to tell you precisely who to follow, as we should all seek out the people that speak to us individually, but I always think the best people to follow are those who give others a platform and who speak about a variety of topics, not just the ones that pertain to them. These are people who utilize their platforms to help liberate others who experience the world in a different way from how they do. They might share their own experience, but also use their platform to highlight the work of others.

While I think social media is a valuable resource for hearing real people's stories and perspectives you might not find via mainstream news sources (like papers or television), we have to be careful and make sure we aren't *just* getting our news via social media. Think about it – when you're scrolling on your phone, how switched on are you to what you're seeing? Are you really paying attention and thinking critically, like you might do if you were reading a book? Or are you also watching TV at the same time? Or even sitting on your phone while chatting with friends?

We scroll, scroll, scroll, and for something to truly catch our attention, it needs to be attention-grabbing. Those who create content on platforms like TikTok and Instagram know this. They want us to be able to instantly understand the point they're making, so complex issues are often condensed down into short, sharp sentences or easily digestible infographics. One quote from an entire interview could be pulled out and shared without the context that surrounded it. Or a major news story – one that has been playing out for years – could be condensed into three simple bullet points that could miss out key details.

Think about it – how often do you hear, 'I saw it on a TikTok,' or 'I read this really powerful Instagram post'? Or how often do you think you know a story because you saw it on your social media? But did you – or the person telling you that information – pause and consider where the facts came from? Or double-check whether the source you are reading or hearing was factually accurate? Our lives are so busy that often we simply don't have time to consider the truth behind what we see online and, because it's easier, simply take it as fact. We absorb information mindlessly, and misinformation can easily be spread online.

It's really important to always keep in mind that . . .

Not everything you see online is true.

We need to remember to question everything we are seeing online. Social media companies do have *some* policies in place to fact-check posts but they're not always reliable, so it's up to us to make sure we're getting our news from a wide array of sources and that – if we see something on social media – we double-check it.

If you see something that piques your interest online, pause and consider . . .

- Where has this come from? Is there a link to the source?
- Can you then check that source? Have a read of the full story and check to see how any quotes or facts fit into the wider story.
- Who would benefit from this information being out there? If the post is taking aim at a particular person or organization, who might benefit from that? What are their political beliefs and stances? What sort of information have they shared before?
- Are there missing voices and perspectives to consider?

As a general rule, if you see something that interests you on any platform, use that as a jumping-off point to read further, rather than taking it as gospel.

We also need to think about this before sharing things on our own social media channels. When there are news stories that make you feel angry or upset, it can be easy to see something online that relates to how you are feeling and share it without thinking. However, we should always take a pause and look beyond our social media feeds to figure out why we are seeing this and whether it's definitely true.

When used carefully, social media can be such a useful tool for sharing information, resources and your own personal experiences. It can be a great starting point to widen your knowledge on a topic and to open important conversations.

Remember earlier, when I asked you to examine if there are any news stories that make you feel angry, or upset? It's absolutely valid if you found those stories via social media, but it's when we rely on it and see it as our only – and main – source of information that problems can arise.

There's only one you! Finding your authenticity

Let's say you know what cause you want to shout about, and you've done your research to give you the confidence to talk about this with conviction. How do you then go about having these conversations in the most authentic way to you?

Today, I can go to an event, dressed head-to-toe in couture, and talk about politics on the red carpet. I can spend a morning being silly and embracing my inner child, laughing with my friends, and then the afternoon shooting a documentary or preparing for a speech at a trade union conference or at a workplace where I've been hired to discuss trans rights and better practices for LGBTQIA+ employees. I can live a life where I get to show all the different sides to myself. I also know that when I do speak up about a cause I care about, I am doing so because it *matters*, not just because I think it will make me look good to the outside world.

There was a time when I didn't feel this way. I thought I couldn't embrace the joys of fashion *and* care deeply about politics and the future of our world. I thought I had to be one thing all the time in order to succeed. It's really easy to fall into this trap, particularly in the early stages of discovering your cause and what you want to talk about. You could be pulled in a totally different direction from what feels right for you, as you see that's where everyone else is going. Or you could, like I did, throw all of your energy into an issue while neglecting all the other parts of yourself that make you, *you*.

That's why, at this stage, I want you to think about what feels right and authentic to you. Once you've identified what cause lights you up, it's worth pausing and considering why you've chosen that cause. Ask yourself:

- Does it feel true to who you are? Or are you just pursuing a cause because it's what everyone else around you is doing?
- Are you embracing all sides of yourself?
- Are you crafting an identity that feels more like a costume than your true self?

To unpick this, it's important to be able to recognize the influence of everything that surrounds you – from the messaging you see on social media, to what you hear your friends talking about. These things can impact you in ways you might not be aware of until you pull back and examine them.

Personal branding

You might have heard the phrase 'personal branding' – it's spoken about a lot when it comes to picking a career, but also when it comes to establishing a presence on social media. At its core, personal branding is the process of defining and promoting what you stand for as an individual. This stretches from how you portray yourself on your CV to what you choose to post about on your Instagram and TikTok (if you choose to have social media).

Branding is a concept that was originally for marketing products, not people. Products can just be one thing . . . humans cannot. I am a model, an activist and a lover of fashion. Like all human beings I am not consistent in what I like and dislike, and I'm sure you are the same. Yet, for a while, I thought my personal brand had to be activism, and activism only.

This is especially the case on social media. There's a risk that internet activism and online conversations can be one-directional, with people just putting their opinions out there and not listening to others. It's so easy to get sucked into that, especially as how social media functions – and therefore how you function within it – is down to how the algorithms are geared. Algorithms are pattern based. They work like a digital librarian, sifting through online content, examining what you've liked in the past and who you follow. They then begin to serve you the content that they think that you are interested in. So, if you like a lot of fashion posts, that will be what you begin to see in your feed. It's useful in some ways, as they can help you find new people to follow or new music to discover by making some accurate guesses as to what you'll like. However, when it comes to us, as human beings existing online, they can flatten us. They can make us focus on one thing, and one thing only.

I thought if I showed the world (and the algorithm) only that side of myself – an activist using their platform for activism alone – I would flourish. But it was the moment that I decided to showcase who I am as a whole person that I really stepped into my power. I saw that I could use fashion and beauty alongside my activism and advocacy, let my guard down and show a softer, more personal side to myself to really allow my voice to be heard. I became much more authentic in who I was.

On social media and beyond, authenticity is really the thing that changes things. Once you get past the need to look a certain way to other people and for other people, you are left with what makes you uniquely you.

Authenticity brands itself.

Whenever anything takes us away from a space of authenticity and into a space of performance is when conversations become hollow and unhelpful. There's only one you. Your individuality and what makes you uniquely you is where your power lies. There will always be people with a similar perspective to you, but you're the only one who has your lived experience. Your voice is integral to change. Why? Because if we hear as many different, unfiltered perspectives as possible, then we get closer to the truth. We can take all of those voices and find a way to create change.

Are you performing?

One Tuesday in June 2020, I opened up my Instagram to see it awash with post after post of the exact same image. Nearly every single thing I scrolled past was a black square – many captioned #blackouttuesday or #blacklivesmatter – and the posts were *supposed* to be a form of collective protest against racism and police brutality.

The movement began within the music industry in response to the murders of George Floyd and Ahmaud Arbery, and the killing of Breonna Taylor. All three were Black Americans who had been killed in 2020. George Floyd was murdered in an act of police brutality when a white police officer, Derek Chauvin, knelt on his neck for over nine minutes while Floyd was handcuffed and lying face-down after being arrested. Breonna Taylor was fatally shot by police officers who forced entry into her home, while Ahmaud Arbery was murdered while out jogging in his neighbourhood, shot in a racially motivated hate crime. Their deaths sparked international outcry and brought conversations – ones that Black people had been having for decades – to a wider audience, as worldwide, people finally began to recognize the racism and brutality that our community faces each day.

As part of this response, two music executives, Brianna Agyemang and Jamila Thomas, launched the Blackout Tuesday initiative and meant it as a call for the music industry to avoid conducting business as usual. In a statement, they wrote, 'Your black executives, artists, managers, staff, colleagues are drained, traumatized, hurt, scared, and angry,' adding, 'I don't want to sit on your Zoom calls talking about the Black artists who are making you so much money if you fail to address what's happening to Black people right now.' They said that 'the show can't just go on, as our people are being hunted and killed.'[4]

But how many people knew all of that history? How many people had that context before they posted the black square on their Instagram feeds? What were they doing behind the scenes? Were they entering into conversations as to how racism functions within society, or were they just hitting 'share' and thinking, '*job done*'?

Performative activism is when you do something because of how it looks, rather than what it achieves, and without taking any *real* action to support the cause.

So many people shared the black square without thinking about why or what it would do, and while it was well intentioned, it didn't actually achieve anything. This is a common problem on social media.

Performative activism is being sucked into a trend without thinking, '*Is this the best use of my platform? The best use of my voice as an activist? Is this actually bringing about change, or am I just performing? Am I doing this so that people think of me in a certain way? Is there more I can be doing beyond this social media post?*' It's OK to give yourself space and time to examine these questions without hitting 'share' right away.

When we are bringing about change and we can see that change happening before our eyes, we feel good about ourselves. When we feel good about what we're doing, it fuels us. It's OK if you feel proud of what you're achieving. But if you are *only* fuelled by the number of people commenting on what you're doing, or what people might think of you, then it can quickly veer into performative activism.

Performative activism looks like:

- adding your voice to a conversation before you've really read up on that topic.
- feeling like you need to respond to something that's happening just because you want people to know that you agree with them.
- wanting people to believe that you know about something . . . before you actually really know about it.
- parroting what other people say without thinking about who they are, why they hold that opinion and why you agree.
- lending your voice to a conversation because it's a 'trendy' topic – not because you really care about it.
- wanting to be seen as 'on the right side' without fully understanding the issue at hand.

You don't need to add your voice to every single cause. And if it's a cause you *do* want to support, your support can take on many forms: it could be volunteering, fundraising, donating, organizing, protesting, or simply bringing people together – there's so much more to be done that isn't just hitting 'share' on a post. What truly matters is that we are informed and active, not just well intentioned and reactive.

Take a moment to think about what action will make a real, tangible impact.

Talking points

I know how easy it is to feel pulled in many different directions and be unsure where to begin when it comes to bringing about change. I understand it can make you feel overwhelmed.

Digging deep into myself and finding my cause, then having conversations and learning more about these issues has brought me so much joy. I feel proud of everything I've achieved and know, deep down, that my voice is making a difference. I want you to feel this way too. And I know that you can.

Remember . . .

- **Activism is a machine.** Once you find your place in it, you can begin to focus your energies on what really makes a difference, rather than feeling that all fires have to be tackled by you and you alone.

- **Information is your biggest asset.** Start reading widely and searching beyond what you're told. Tune your brain to always be aware of what information might be missing and who else's voice needs to be heard. Then seek it out.

- **Be authentically you.** Don't dilute any part of yourself, and remember to ask yourself if you're doing work that feels good because you're proud of what it can achieve, or if you're just performing for others.

2

We Need to Talk About . . . Community

Together, as a community, we can find new ways to exist.

Often when people hear the word 'community', they think of their neighbourhood, where they live or where they grew up. But that's not what I mean when I say 'community'. I didn't find my community where I was born – I found it by leaving and meeting new people, others who I could see myself and my experiences mirrored in.

For me, community is the earth where you put down your roots, and it's ever-changing and evolving, with new people coming and going. So, don't worry if you don't feel like you have a community around you just yet, as for a long time, I didn't either.

Growing up, I genuinely thought I was the only person like me. It was the most heartbreaking thing. The fear of how alone I felt in the world kept me silent. When we're hidden, we hide. But as I was one of the very few Black and openly queer people in my small town, I was both isolated but incredibly visible. It's why it took me finding my community in those early university years to finally find my voice.

It was the first time I could look around and see people like me who felt the same way about the world as I did. I began to open up and share my opinions, as I felt safe to do so. This is why I want you to find your community and start conversations from there. By talking to your peers and people who you can see yourself in, you'll begin to feel safe and confident in growing and expanding your opinions.

Once you can understand and recognize that there are people out there like you, you can then seek them out and begin to ask questions. There will be people and places out there that light you up and make you feel like your true self. They feel like home, even if you are far away from where you were born.

I want to help you find that home for yourself.

For me, I've always felt myself in queer spaces. I remember being 16 and a friend sneaking me into a nightclub in Soho for the first time. Growing up I'd always had this sense of shame instilled into me, as though I was the only queer person alive and queer people were merely an ideology, not a reality – yet all of sudden, here I was surrounded by thousands of them. There were so many characters and people that were living beyond the parameters of what I had been told by the world was 'acceptable'. It made me feel like being camp and effeminate wasn't wrong. These spaces offered me a chance to live without self-censorship.

Now, I find that – whether it's an LGBTQIA+ centre, a gay bar or a club – when I step into a queer space it's as if I have entered a place of universal understanding. Like we're all speaking the same language in a culture that goes beyond words. The energy in these spaces is nourishing and accepting in a way that wider society isn't. At the beginning of my transition being in these places offered me fleeting moments of 'this makes me feel good', and 'this space feels like a refuge'. While at first I felt I had to rely on community for that feeling, eventually I began to carry that sense of self and home within me everywhere I went.

There are also communities within communities. You don't need to belong to just one, because we as individuals contain multitudes. Finding your community is about seeking it out in the different places that satisfy the different parts of us. That could look like . . .

● **intentionally thinking about your interests.** This is a great place to start and you could also combine your interests with your identity. Say you're queer and interested in playing a sport – you could search for a queer or trans sports team and see if there are any local groups in your area. Or if a book or writing club is more your thing, you can also look online, and many independent book shops will have notice boards advertising meetups.

- **looking into political organizations.** You'll find people of all ages and from all backgrounds who believe in a common cause. Even if you simply sign up to a party's website, they will send you events, campaigns and opportunities to get involved and meet new people.

- **going to protests.** You'll hear me talk a lot in this book about the power of protests for so many different reasons, and one of them is that they're a great place to find your community. Go along and you'll find every single different type of person all united by fighting for or speaking out against one cause. You'll find lots of people go to protests on their own (but do make sure you follow any safety protocols – these are often found on the social media pages of the protests).

- **focusing on your cause.** Revisit the cause that you discovered in Chapter 1 and try and find events or places where others who care about that thing might congregate. If LGBTQIA+ rights is an area of focus for you, you could find your local queer bookshop and see what events they have on. Or if the environment and climate change is one of your passions, are there any activist groups nearby that you could join?

Finding new ways, together

When I was 24 years old, I experienced how communities can come together to make a big change. I met my friends Nadine Noor and Skye Cooper Barr, who were looking to form a collective – a group that encompassed femmes (a queer person who presents femininely) from all different walks of life. Their aim was to bring us together and combat what was, at the time, an incredibly toxic nightlife culture.

Clubs and the nightlife scene back then often didn't feel like safe places to go and dance. Women were objectified and constantly hit on, with 'no' rarely being taken for an answer. Dark-skinned Black women were also being routinely refused entry to nightclubs because those who ran the clubs felt they weren't the 'right' kind of women they wanted in their space.

We wanted to counter that culture. We wanted to create a space where we could be free and empowered. We wanted to be able to wear what we wanted to wear, knowing that we were in a safer space. We came together to discuss how we could create that space, and soon PXSSY PALACE was formed.

We held events across London, and it was a place for people who didn't feel comfortable in traditional nightclub settings – usually because of their sexuality, gender identity, body shape or any other reason. They could come and feel comfortable with us. We called it a safer space, where safety came before everything else. We put together a code of conduct that was paramount – there would be no homophobia, transphobia, ableism, racism, religious intolerance, disablism or body shaming. If someone did experience one of those things on our nights, then the person responsible would be thrown out straight away. It's how all clubs and night-time venues should be, but from our experiences, that wasn't how they were operating.

PXSSY PALACE played a huge role in changing the landscape of queer nightlife in London, and it then spread. Now PXSSY PALACE has been all over the world – from Amsterdam to Australia – but I also see how it has inspired so many other raves that are on the scene today. Queer nightlife in particular holds similar codes of conduct to those that we created, with the safety and freedom of the guests inside paramount. I'm incredibly proud to have played a small part in PXSSY PALACE's legacy, which continues to inspire and empower new generations of queer ravers. It's where my activism truly began, alongside Nadine, Skye, Kesang, Bemi, Sophie and Alexa.

We can create the communities that we want to see.

People met at PXSSY PALACE and began their own collectives and their own communities. Once you find the space that feels like home – somewhere that lights you up – you know it and you will want more of that space and the people in it. You'll feel empowered by those around you to continue being yourself. We found that by creating a space of safety where like-minded people could meet, it gave so many others the spark and inspiration they needed to know that change was possible. These people weren't just throwing parties – they were also hosting panel talks and creating spaces and platforms for people to share their stories and experiences.

All of what was achieved came from us coming together due to our shared experiences and discussing what we didn't like about the world we lived in. From there we could talk and listen to each other to help find solutions together. It all began with a conversation.

How to be an ally

Think about a time when you felt safe to be yourself. Were you in a certain place? Or was it less to do with the physical space you were in and more to do with the people that you were with? Remember how I said earlier that I carry with me a sense of refuge, one that makes me feel safe in myself no matter where I am? I couldn't have reached that state without the support of the people around me who made me feel like I could be entirely myself around them.

That's what it means to be an ally – showing that *you* are a safe space for people.

Being an ally is about taking the initiative to understand how you can engage with issues of injustice even though you aren't directly impacted by them. It's about proactively seeking out opportunities to address issues as they evolve. It's about lending your voice to a cause in order to support others. Allies are vital members of communities. At its core, allyship is empathy in action.

An ally . . .

- understands that change comes about through *doing*.
- knows that it's not just about *thinking* that people deserve equality, respect, dignity and justice, but instead understands that it's up to all of us to ensure that change actually happens.
- takes the time to understand the reality of those around them.
- uses their power to allow others to speak.

An ally is a person who creates a space of freedom.

This will mean different things for different people. Take the trans experience – not all trans experiences are the same, and it isn't always possible to simply go up to someone and ask them what they need. When I was growing up, if someone had asked me what I needed, I wouldn't have known what to say, and I could only recognize that further along in my journey.

So, when I say that an ally is a safe space for people, this involves trying to proactively learn about other people's reality. You need to be switched on and aware of both the current climate we're living in and what has happened in the past. You can take that knowledge and use it to try and empathize with how someone might be experiencing the world in a different way from you.

Active allyship

Have a look around you in your school, college, university or workplace. What current structures are in place, and how could they make others feel? Look at what exists that might benefit some while putting others at a disadvantage, and question what you could do to change that. Most of the institutions that we learn or work in will tend to have policies in place that are there – in theory – to protect the people who go there each day. But often these policies have been created by a select few people at the top who could be carrying their own biases and prejudices.

Much like how you examined historical texts and identified the missing voices, you could do the same here. Whose voices, experiences, needs or perspectives aren't being reflected or accommodated?

There are so many things that you may not initially notice that can create barriers for others. For example, if you are not disabled, you may not be aware of how an absence of sloped kerbs and ramps or a lift that's consistently out of order could impact someone who experiences challenges with their mobility from freely moving around. We all experience spaces in a different way and some may struggle more than others.

Taking the time to consider what those around you might need to feel safe and heard plays such a vital role in activism. If we aren't working together then nothing changes. Ultimately it's about asking:

- Are all areas fully accessible?
- When it comes to talks, are all viewpoints and backgrounds being considered?
- Who are the people running the school, college, university or workplace you attend? Might they hold some biases that mean they are excluding certain voices and experiences?
- Are the events accommodating people with neurodivergent brains who might struggle in loud, busy environments?

And it's not just these tangible, physical things that you need to consider in order to be an ally. Sometimes, for instance, an influx of a certain type of news story can have a huge impact on people. As I'm writing, there's a lot of transphobia in the news, which results in transgender people feeling more unsafe to be themselves. Other examples of the impact of these kinds of news stories include how refugees can sometimes be spoken about in the news or on social media in a negative and dehumanizing way. If a refugee family moved to your area or there was a new student joining your school, how could that messaging impact how they behave?

Once you've thought about the hurdles that someone might be facing that could be stopping them from being themselves, you can ask yourself . . .

- What can I do to make them feel more comfortable?
- How could I make someone feel more welcome?

Take something like putting a Pride flag in your window or wearing a pin badge showcasing your beliefs. It seems a small thing, but what it's creating is a general atmosphere of welcome, which is even more important if you're used to seeing the opposite. Of course a flag isn't going to end homophobia or transphobia, but it does help people who feel disenfranchised feel more able to be themselves. It shows you are an ally and a safe space, and it can create a conversation that can only lead to more progress. All of these little things accumulate into a bigger picture.

But once you've done something small, you're going to want to build on that. Wearing badges and pins sends a message, but to be a true ally you'll need to do more. You could . . .

- **Speak to the people in charge.** For example, if there is an accessibility issue, find out who you can reach out to so it can be changed.
- **Lend your time to an organization.** This could involve finding a group linked to the passion you identified in Chapter 1 or thinking about what is needed in your community. Is there a soup kitchen, local charity or food bank nearby that could do with your help?

- **Use your skills.** Say you're really good at art or design – could you help to design pamphlets or posters for a protest? Or if you're good at numbers or organization, could you help a local charity with their admin? Find the contact details of an organization and reach out and ask how best you can help them. Often smaller charities or groups are more likely to respond and need help.
- **Become a protest steward.** Many marches and rallies need stewards, to help keep people safe and make sure the events go off without a hitch. Trans Pride, for example, is growing each year and always needs volunteer stewards. It gives information about how to apply on its social media page.
- **Share information on social media.** If you have a platform and want to advocate for different organizations, follow them and share their information on your own page to let others know about the work that they do.

Really the list of what you could do to be an ally is endless. It's about using your imagination and thinking of the skills you have that a cause or organization might need. You'll have to take some initiative, but you will find that once you begin to get involved everything that you can do will become so much clearer.

A great example of allyship is when students have come together to fight against discriminatory uniform policies. In London in 2021, students that attended Pimlico Academy protested against the school introducing new rules that banned colourful hijabs and hairstyles that 'block the views' of others.[5] Or, in 2017, Chikayzea Flanders was placed in isolation after starting at secondary school because his dreadlocks were deemed to be in breach of the school's uniform policy.[6] For so long, the emphasis on resisting school uniform policies like these was placed on students and their families – in Flanders's case his mother took out legal action – but through campaigning and protests, new guidelines were put in place in 2022 that state that pupils who wear their hair in natural Afro styles will be protected by law. To reach this place took a community effort from pupils, parents, teachers and those who work within human rights to all come together and keep demanding and pushing for change.

We are stronger as a community.

Talking points

Your community is comforting, but it should also challenge you – *gently* and in a way that makes you feel safe. You can also be that person for other people. We should all feel free to expand our minds and learn together. Finding your community and recognizing all the different voices within it is so powerful. We can gain confidence from one another.

Remember . . .

- **Your community is out there, I promise.** You'll find it by stepping into new spaces, seeking out like-minded people and starting conversations.
- **We all need a safe space.** Don't underestimate your power to be a safe space, both for yourself and for other people.
- **Allies are integral to a community.** Recognize how structures could make those around you stop speaking up. What can we all do to try and change that? What can you do? Inclusivity is so important. We want everyone to feel able to contribute to the conversation.
- **Small seeds create bigger change.** Even the tiniest of actions (like asking a question or checking in on someone) could be noticed and make someone feel better. That, in turn, could create a ripple effect where they feel able to speak up and bring about their own small seeds of change. From there, a better world can grow.

Part 2

How to Speak Up

It was an immense sense of frustration with the way the world was that led me to first start talking about my experiences publicly in 2014. This frustration came from so many different places – from seeing transphobic storylines in comedy films where our experiences were openly mocked, to the overwhelming sense that people believed we should live in the shadows and never speak up about our realities.

For a few years, it felt like all of that was about to change. It was a hopeful time. We had Laverne Cox, who was starring in Netflix's biggest drama of the time – *Orange Is the New Black* – becoming the first trans woman to be nominated for an Emmy and the first trans woman to appear on the cover of *Time* magazine. The show *Transparent*, which told the story of what it's like to transition later in life, was also airing and being hugely praised. It felt like we were at the heart of a cultural shift that felt powerful and progressive.

I was working as a model and a DJ, and in general my public persona was slowly growing. Through this I was approached to be interviewed for a double-page spread in the British newspaper the *Evening Standard*.[7] It was an opportunity for me to share my experiences, and the article opened doors for me – it gave me a chance to speak and have my voice heard.

Yet even from that spread, it was clear how much more had to be done, as, within the article, they called me 'London's own Laverne Cox'. Laverne has always been a source of power for me, as she is for many trans people, but it was a sign of how limited trans representation was. Laverne and I live very different lives – the only thing we have in common is that we are both Black trans women. It reflected how things were at the time (and how things remain in many ways) as so often society views all trans people as the same. My transness was assumed to be the wholeness of my identity, as it was for Laverne, rather than considering that we are two very different people from two very different walks of life.

It became clear from that spread why it was so vital to keep speaking up. One story wasn't enough – I wanted to keep adding my own experience to the discussion and show the world the realities of my life however I could.

The conversations you begin to have might not be as public as mine were, but that doesn't matter – a conversation does not have to go out to a wide audience for it to be important. Instead you can begin by talking to those immediately around you and see where that might lead you all. Whatever your ambitions may be, speaking up and having conversations – whether on a public, professional or more personal level with your friends and family – does make a difference. It helps to spread ideas, and new ways of living and thinking. It can inspire others, and it can show people who perhaps haven't ever considered another way that we don't have to just accept the things in life that cause ourselves or other people harm.

I absolutely believe that change comes about from having conversations with your friends, your family, your community, those who agree with you and those who don't. But it also comes from knowing when to stop talking, when to listen and when to admit that you're wrong.

Are you ready to start talking?

3

We Need to Talk About ... Tricky Conversations

The brilliant thing about finding your cause and the issue that lights you up is that it can make you feel so passionate and *alive*. The tough thing? When we're passionate about something, we will encounter people who don't feel the same way as us who will challenge us and want us to be wrong. Of course, not every conversation you have will be tricky. There will be so many that are just an exchange of information when you're both in a place to learn from each other. But there will be some that are challenging. This could be because there's a great deal of pressure on you to deliver – for example, if you're asked to give a speech or record a video on something you care about. Or it could be that they're challenging because they're close to home. Conversations that you need to have with friends and family when you don't see eye to eye on an issue can sometimes be the trickiest of all.

In all conversations, there are moments where it would be so easy to let your nerves or emotions run away with you. I've felt that flutter in my stomach so often. But I've had enough of these conversations now to know that to be a successful public speaker or debater – or even just someone who can calmly get their point across in heated debates with family and friends – takes practice. So much of what I'll be sharing in this chapter comes from years of tricky conversations, both in public and in private.

As part of my career as an activist, I have faced challenging discussions on a public scale, and I have learned so much from these moments that I want to share with you. There may be times you think, '*I'll never do a talk at the UN*' or '*Well I don't plan on embarking on a career that involves being challenged on breakfast television.*' The thing is, you don't know what lies ahead and the lessons I've learned from these moments are just as relevant to the tough conversations I've had privately with people I know.

I've had to have many tough discussions with friends and family, and I have found the way that I prepare for the more public conversations also helps prepare me for the more private. Of course, every situation is different, and you aren't going to go through a rigorous amount of research and prepping just to have a small chat with a friend! However, the more you apply these principles of thinking to *all* your conversations, the more you'll get to know yourself, your triggers and your cause so much better.

Why do conversations get tricky?

If you want to bring about change, you have to be prepared to be challenged. You can't be afraid of it or see being challenged as a failure on your part. Throughout history, change has always been resisted and many important things we now take as standard parts of life were once fought for. People recognized that their rights were being restricted, and they came together and shouted – *loudly* – about how wrong it was. And they had many people who challenged them along the way!

Did you know that . . .

● in the eighteenth and nineteenth centuries, women could be jailed for wearing trousers in the UK, the US and France?[8]
● until 1967, it was illegal to be a gay man in England and Wales?[9]
● in certain parts of America, up until the mid 1960s, there was a racial caste system known as Jim Crow that upheld etiquette norms that stopped Black and white people from eating together? Schools, toilets, libraries, public transport, parks, restaurants and water fountains were segregated.[10]

These are just a tiny handful of examples of the way laws and social norms oppressed marginalized people within society throughout history.

There are so many others, and, as discussed in the earlier chapters, it's vital that you do your own research. Huge historical events can't be distilled into just one or two lines, particularly as their impact remains in how we live our lives today. And while the fact that these laws no longer remain in place today is a sign of progress, there's still so much more to be done. For example, there are still 65 countries that have laws that criminalize homosexuality, and there are many places across the world where women are punished for how they dress.

I mention these examples because I often draw power through looking back in history and seeing what has changed. But also to remind myself to constantly be challenging and questioning our current social norms and laws. When you look at the list on the previous page it's important to ask yourself:

- Why were these laws there in the first place?
- Who did they benefit?
- What group in society wanted them to be upheld?
- Why would some people have not wanted change?

If things have been comfortable for one group of people for a long time, they won't want things to change. This could come from people benefitting financially from the rules in place, or it could be that change – at its essence – challenges individuals to examine their own identities and lives. Us speaking out shows a new way of being, and this could be scary, as it shows people that things could be about to change (or that they should).

So, people might push back. They might try to silence our stories, make us feel stupid and wrong, or even strip back our rights. This can be exhausting for those of us who want – and need – change to happen. We can feel worn out by the fight of it all. But I've found that looking back at what people fought for in the past and how they received the same reactions but pushed through can really help galvanize me today.

Take Section 28, the law I grew up under. It was passed in 1988 – two years after I was born – in the UK by the Conservative government that was in power at the time. It stopped councils and schools from 'promoting homosexuality'. This meant teachers couldn't discuss same-sex relationships, or show us plays, books or films that discussed homosexuality. It was in place from 1988 to 2000 in Scotland, and to 2003 in England and Wales.[11]

Before Section 28 came into place the gay rights movement was making (some) strides, and there was much more awareness of LGBTQIA+ rights. Gay people – men in particular – were sharing their stories, and there had been a reversal on laws that criminalized homosexuality. But then Margaret Thatcher, who was the prime minister at the time, came along and said in a speech, 'Children who need to be taught to respect traditional moral values are being taught that they have an inalienable right to be gay.'[12]

Homophobia was being painted as keeping kids 'safe' from 'corruption of the mind'. It was this nonsensical idea that you could somehow stamp out a child's sexuality by prohibiting them from having access to information or assistance. We have seen from Section 28's legacy that it does not work. Queer kids did not become straight – all it did was lead to a generation of traumatized queer adults. I needed support and to be able to see myself in culture to know that I was not alone. Instead, Section 28 added to my deep feelings of alienation.

Today when we look at the discussions surrounding trans people and our rights, what's happening is incredibly similar to Section 28 and the conversations it sparked. As I said, when I started speaking out in 2014, it felt like a hopeful time . . . more and more of us were finding our voice. Powerful figures do not like this, and we are now seeing them pushing back, in a myriad of different, frightening ways. They have tried to limit our access to public spaces, with former prime minister Rishi Sunak pledging to rewrite the Equality Act to define 'sex' as meaning biological sex (meaning trans women would not be allowed to use women's toilets), while Keir Starmer has previously said that trans women with gender recognition certificates 'don't' and 'shouldn't' have the right to use female-only spaces.[13] In 2024 the Conservative government drafted guidance to stop schools from teaching the concept of gender identity.[14]

This is just one of many examples of how whenever people become visible and begin fighting for their rights, there will always be those who try to oppose and fight against them.

This can sometimes feel like we're stuck in a loop, like nothing is changing. But *it is*. You can see that from all the change that's happened throughout history. Section 28 ended in 2003, and there have been so many other huge strides made for LGBTQIA+ rights since, such as same-sex couples being able to legally get married in 38 countries, and laws like the UK's Gender Recognition Act 2004 being passed, which gives trans people a way to change their gender. So much confidence can be found in the progression of human acceptance.

But that doesn't make it easy. It's exhausting to face this push-back when all we are advocating for is the right to live happy, safe lives. The way that trans people are spoken about by powerful figures across the world has had a huge impact on my mental health and that of my community. I can't lie and pretend these conversations will always be easy. But change *can* happen and continues to.

Remind yourself of this if you're ever in need of a 'why' to keep you going.

How to prepare for a tricky conversation

Remember, you're probably more prepared than you think. When we're passionate about things, we absorb so much, and it's more than likely you'll have already read and discovered lots about whatever it is you're planning on speaking about. But saying that, I am a big believer in preparing for tricky conversations as much as you can. This preparation doesn't just involve knowing your topic, but also thinking about what challenges you might face. If you're debating someone, it's worth considering what your opponent could say and what might throw you off course. You need to examine how you've talked about certain subjects in the past, looking at and learning from where you got it right and where you got it wrong.

The thing is, nothing ever goes entirely perfectly. There will always be so many different variables involved, and you can't control your environment or how people will respond to you. What you *can* control is your mindset, your preparation and how much you are on your own side.

I'm going to talk you through a few examples of big talks I've given in my life so you can see what preparation looks like for me. It doesn't follow the exact same pattern every single time, and it certainly isn't as rigorous when it's a more personal conversation (more on those later), but I do tend to ensure that before any big conversation, I have . . .

- reminded myself that I can do it.
- prepared what I'm going to say and how.
- planned for any 'gotcha' moments.
- thought about how to channel my nerves and emotions.

You can do it

One of my most memorable talks was in 2022 at the United Nations Headquarters in New York. The UN is one of the biggest international organizations, and it brings together people from across the globe to gather, discuss common problems and endeavour to find shared solutions that benefit all of humanity. Its work is so important and it was one of the biggest moments of my entire career. As someone who was speaking for my community – people who so often aren't heard – there was no better place to talk about trans rights than the UN, where I would be heard by world leaders who are in positions of power and can drive big changes that would directly help us. I remember feeling really calm beforehand – it was a surreal feeling. I even said to myself, '*You really should be a lot more nervous than you actually are.*' But in a way, I'd been preparing for this moment for the whole of my adult life. I'd learned from my past to find belief in myself and that brought this sense of calm.

When I first began in activism, before I'd go on stage to give a talk, I would look at a situation and think, '*Everyone here wants me to fail.*' It was not a healthy mindset. If you get into that way of thinking, it's really easy to convince yourself that there's no point in preparing, as you're never going to be good enough. But you *are* good enough.

You must make sure you're not the one getting in your own way.

If you constantly tell yourself you're going to fail then it's much harder to succeed. Now, before I give a talk or when I know I'll be entering into a tough conversation, I remind myself . . .

- **I am doing this for a reason.** I have an important message to share, and even if my message connects with just one person, I have succeeded.
- **I know what I am talking about, and people want to learn from me.** This is a kind reminder and puts me in a good headspace. I tell myself people are there to get something that they either want or need to learn from me and hear what I have to say.
- **It's OK if people aren't on my side.** It's inevitable that people aren't going to always agree with me. But in these scenarios, I use it as fuel and tell myself to 'prove them wrong'.

My talk at the UN was discussing the need for a dismantling of stereotypes in advertisements and the media. I was pushing the idea that we shouldn't settle for the way that we as trans people are represented. I felt strong in why I was discussing this, and I knew who I was speaking for and to. I felt so confident in my ability to deliver, and this confidence was key to getting me in the right headspace to give this important talk.

Prepare . . . but don't be too rigid

When I first started public speaking, I was so wrapped up with nerves that I wouldn't be able to keep my train of thought. But over time I've come to accept that about myself and embrace that it's part of who I am. Battling with myself and trying to stop myself from going off on tangents was making me too anxious, so instead I now try and tell myself that often the best stuff comes from going off on these unexpected angles – as long as you bring the audience back to the main point at the end.

I do this by going into more professional discussions (we will go into more casual talks later) with a structure for the conversation. This will look different for everyone – for some it could just be brief bullet points of what you want to talk about, whereas for others, it could be much more detailed notes. It could also be a script, but for me this doesn't work as well as I like to adjust how I speak depending on the audience.

For example, during Pride month I give a lot of talks to people in the workplace about my experiences and what trans people need from their employers, which also often brings in discussions of racism as well. If I go into the room and it is full of people who experience racism, transphobia or homophobia, I won't explain their own lived experience back to them. So although the overall message always stays the same, I adapt what I talk about and how I deliver my speech depending on the audience.

With practice you will get a lot better at thinking on your feet, but having a rough idea of what you want to cover and your main point is very useful preparation for any conversation.

Gotcha! Or did they . . .?

Before I go into any conversation or debate, I think about who I'm speaking to and try to work out what their angle or argument with me could be, and – in some cases – how I think they might be trying to catch me out. It's what I call their 'gotcha' moment – a point that someone who disagrees with me wants to trip me up on. If it's a journalist, this 'gotcha' moment could also be them trying to get me to say something controversial that could make their headline punchier. Even if you're not talking about your subject in such a public way, there will always be people who will disagree with you and want you to fumble or mess up your point.

With the talk at the UN, I was aware that trans representation had moved forward since I first started speaking about my experience, but I also knew that we still have a long way to go. I expected that there could be people in the crowd who would think that the progress we'd made was 'enough'. I thought of my counter to that, which was to remind them that the conversation is consistently evolving and so now the goalposts have changed.

Now that we have more visibility, we need to challenge what that visibility looks like and whether it expresses the reality of trans people. With time, we've come to see that visibility doesn't necessarily keep trans people safe – hate crimes are on the rise, and there have been news stories in the UK, the US and in many other countries that showcase how their police forces have displayed transphobic behaviours.[15] I wanted to convey how important it is that we are constantly pushing for better representation of trans people for true equality and to protect their safety.

I was conscious that people might try and catch me out, so I thought carefully about how to frame my argument. Here's how you can prepare and think about what your 'gotcha' moment might be:

- **Look into who you're speaking to, or who will be in the room with you.** Do you know what their opinions on this subject are already? Can you dig into their backgrounds or beliefs? You could see what they've shared on social media, or if they've written something for their own blog or newsletter.
- **Think about what their argument might be and how they could 'get' you.** You could look into the opinions and arguments of people with similar views to them and the points they tend to make. Then think about how to counter them. Say you're speaking to someone who believes that climate change has been over-exaggerated. You could look up examples of natural disasters and look into statistics that show these events really aren't 'ordinary' occurrences but are the result of climate change.
- **Consider how it could get personal.** I've found that often when people want to trip you up during a discussion, they will move the conversation away from the topic at hand and instead move towards personal points. They

know that's what's going to upset you or make you angry and therefore might derail your argument. If you know there's a likelihood that will happen, you won't be as thrown off guard and you can pivot the question back to the point you want to make.

I remember once I was invited on breakfast television to discuss a doctor who had been fired for saying that people can't choose their gender. But instead of that remaining the focus, the television host proceeded to ask me over and over again what gender it says on my passport. It was so personal and completely off the point of the discussion, and in the moment, I was thrown. I wanted to ask, 'How dare you?' It was so insulting to be asked such a personal question, and I was angry that there was this assumption that a piece of state documentation is the sole indicator of who I actually am.

It reduced my humanity to a piece of paper. But I knew that responding angrily would give him exactly what he wanted from me and take up the time I could instead use to get my point across. I had to very quickly pull myself back from my anger. I had to keep repeating that who I am has nothing to do with a piece of paper, bringing it back to the argument at hand rather than derailing the conversation by answering his question.

Moments like this were so common in the early days of my career. In many ways, every public conversation I took part in felt like one big 'gotcha' moment. I was constantly having to make people see my humanity and convince them that it wasn't that I *thought* I was a woman; it was that I *am* a woman. 'Gotcha' moments can be incredibly tough to navigate, but the key thing is to redirect the questions away from the personal and back to the topic at hand.

It's also important to recognize that if someone does try to trip you up with a 'gotcha' moment, it speaks more about them than it does you. We see this happening all the time with climate activist Greta Thunberg, who was 15 when she first began protesting about climate change. We see how her opponents will use how she looks, her age and how she is perceived as ways of invalidating what she is trying to say. But in fact it really just weakens her opponents' case as it shows how they are not listening to what she has to say and that they don't have a strong enough argument to retaliate.

Handling your nerves and emotions

I've also found some very helpful ways to train myself in keeping calm and in the moment. The UN building I was speaking in was in New York. I knew how huge a moment this was going to be and so I made sure to plan things around the talk that I knew would help me control my mind and reactions as much as possible.

I touched down the night before and went straight to the gym before having an early night. When I woke up that morning, I felt a little nervous, and whenever I feel nerves, I find a good way to get rid of them is to place the focus back into my body. Moving my body and connecting with my breath re-centres me. One of the worst things you can do when you're feeling that jangling, nervous, anxious feeling is to sit in it. It's vital to change your environment to get out of your mind and into your body. For me, that looks like getting up and going to the gym.

But for you changing your environment might look different. Perhaps you prefer to step outside to absorb some sunshine or fresh air, or speak to a friend. Whichever way works best for you, it's a good idea to take that emotion and shift it elsewhere to change your feelings into something positive and productive.

In fact, I learned this skill of taking a negative emotion and using it to power me forward from walking the runway. Walking a runway is an extremely difficult thing to do. I liken the experience to being told to pick up a pen, but make it look natural, then do it with a camera on you, and then do it three more times! It's an odd feeling and a huge pressure, so the only thing you can do before walking a runway is take those nerves and turn them into focus. I'd say to myself . . .

'Instead of feeling nervous, I'm going to feel fierce, I'm going to feel driven and I'm going to do what people came here to see me do.'

I did the same before the UN speech.

Walking into the room, with its stark silence, was so daunting. I was so aware of my breath and each movement I was making. No matter how much preparation you do, you never know how you'll feel stepping into a new environment, particularly such a high-pressured one where all eyes are on you. But I knew I had to trust myself, and to trust that I knew what I was talking about and that I was prepared. And I was. I was proud of my speech that day – it was a huge moment in my career, and since then I've been appointed as the first UN Women UK Champion.

But despite the talk going so well, of course, afterwards, I analysed and was critical of myself. I knew I wanted to keep speaking on world stages about so many different topics, and that each opportunity I took was a chance to learn and improve. This attitude is one of the reasons I have managed to harness a feeling of calm before each speaking opportunity – I know that I am constantly growing and learning.

Know yourself

Have you ever watched yourself speaking back on video? Maybe you've listened to a voice note you recorded for a friend, or watched a social media reel that you made? It can be really tough to analyse yourself – you may just want to hide your eyes behind your hands or throw your phone across the room. But a big part of growing my confidence in tough conversations involved being hyper-analytical of myself. If I've been on television or one of my speeches has been recorded, I will watch myself back. I want to use my own performance to keep learning more about myself, how I currently communicate and how I want to communicate in the future.

I'm in a unique position as I do have access to a lot of my speeches and television appearances, and this may not be possible for you. One thing you could do if you're making a speech is ask a friend, teacher, or parent or carer to record you so then you can watch it back. Or, if you've not made a public speech but still want to take some time to learn from a conversation you had, you can do this without a recording too. Take some time after the conversation to reflect. You could make notes or just think about how you did. You can reflect on the moments you didn't feel so sure of yourself and why, and you can also think about what went well and which parts of the conversation you thought were successful. Maybe you felt you made a strong argument, or you could tell that the other person was coming around to your point of view. If that was the case, how did you achieve that? If a friend is there – someone who you can trust will be honest – you could also ask them what they thought too.

When I do this, I ask myself questions like:

- How well did I form my argument?
- How well did I connect with the audience?
- What was my body language saying?
- Could I have offered better context?
- How quickly could I pull my facts out?

- Who else could I have referenced when making that point?
- Did I use this as an opportunity to platform my community in the most effective way?

These are things I can actually build and improve on. But in the past, I found myself straying into unhelpful territory with questions like:

- How did I look in that outfit?
- How was my make-up?
- Did my hair look OK?
- What will people say about me?

Those are questions that put me into a place where I am being cruel to myself. They're also focused on performance – how I *look* to others rather than the purpose of the conversation. The questions I ask myself *have* to be ones that are for the betterment of my cause. They are tough questions, but they are rooted in the need to want to be better, so they're worth asking. The others aren't necessary, as they're focusing on things that, in the grand scheme of it all, really don't matter.

Of course, it's natural to be concerned by our appearance, as we've been raised in a culture that puts looking a certain way at the forefront of importance. But ultimately if we spend too much time worrying about appearance-based concerns, then we are focusing more on how we're *performing* our activism and not our words themselves.

If I find myself veering into unfairly critical territory, I try to catch myself. I remind myself that it doesn't matter if my hair isn't perfect or my skin isn't flawless. It's easy to run away with these thoughts, so there's great power in catching and rerouting them.

I once appeared on *Loose Women*, a popular UK chat show, to talk about my experience of being sexually assaulted and the state of play for trans rights in the UK. My hair got stuck in my lapel microphone, which pulled it across my chest. It was so easy to get distracted by this tiny thing, but I told myself, '*Listen to what you're talking about; listen to what you're doing for your community and for yourself – that's what's important, not this rogue strand of hair. That really doesn't matter. It's hair and it moves.*'

It could be a hair out of place. Or a spot on your face. Or even food in your teeth. These things happen. Don't let it distract you and lower your confidence in yourself, as no one is going to notice. They will be paying attention to the important point you're making. If they do notice, and that's something they care about? Well, that tells you more about them than it does about you.

Preparation looks like . . .

- **knowing your topic as much as possible.** Have you read all sides of the debate and examined the history of it?
- **thinking about your language and tone.** At what points do you want to show your passion? When do you want to bring in personal experience? Will there be times when you just stick to facts?

- **knowing who you're speaking to.** What might they be wanting you to say that will prove them right? Will they have a 'gotcha' moment?
- **examining your past debates or conversations.** Were there moments you let your nerves take over? How did you come across? Were there things you forgot to say? What went well, and how can you achieve that again?

Talking to a bigot

Have you ever found yourself at a party where you're having so much fun, but then someone – perhaps a friend, or even just someone you met that night – says something you know to be offensive? That anxious feeling of dread settles in your stomach as you wonder, *'Should I speak up? Is it my duty?'*

The more engaged we become with the world, the more we can begin to feel like it's our job to be fighting for our causes 24/7. Our desire for a better world can leak into everything we do, and we can feel like we have failed in the instances when we sense we should have spoken up but didn't. However, you can't change everyone's mind, and other people's opinions and thoughts are not your responsibility, particularly if by saying something you could be putting your or someone else's safety or well-being at risk. You can just remove yourself from a group or situation, or – if you feel you're able to – you could disagree *while* removing yourself by saying something along the lines of, 'This conversation is making me feel uncomfortable and what you're saying is offensive, so I'm going to remove myself.'

If you *do* want to speak up against someone being bigoted or offensive, then don't feel that you have to be completely knowledgeable on a topic in order to call them out. You don't have to know everything about slavery to know that systemic racism is wrong. You don't have to know everything about conflicts in the Middle East to know that people shouldn't be targeted for being who they are, and that human rights should be upheld for all people, regardless of race or religion.

If I hear someone say something I don't agree with, and I want to challenge them on it, I'll consider the following:

- **The environment.** Think about how receptive a person will be to your words, and who else is there. Are there lots of people around them? Will they feel embarrassed and possibly react stubbornly or angrily?
- **Their intention.** Have they said something wilfully ignorant? Or have they spoken without thinking and said something unwittingly offensive? I always consider the energy behind the words, as that helps reframe my response. If someone is intentionally trying to get others' backs up, I often won't waste my energy on them, knowing that they won't truly listen to what I have to say. But if it's someone who has almost accidentally said something wrong then I will try to carefully make them see where they went wrong.

- **How to respond with empathy.** Throughout life, we are *all* going to make mistakes and get things wrong. The things that we thought ten years ago may not be what we think now. We have to have empathy for those that we speak to, remembering that as humans, we're all massively flawed individuals who are capable of both awful and amazing things.

Changing someone's mind

It's also important that in these conversations we allow people to be wrong and we allow them to change their minds. Of course, there are those who commit atrocities and people who are disproportionately awful to others, but most of the time, it's OK to make mistakes and it's OK to change your mind. If we expect others to allow that of us, we have to offer them the same understanding and grace.

If we aren't allowing people to change their minds, then why are we even talking?

When I have tough conversations with people, I want them to come around to a different way of thinking. Think of a journalist, influencer or television pundit who has very strong views that you disagree with. Now imagine that, one day, they turn around and say, 'I've balanced things up, and I feel like the entire time I've been getting it wrong. I'm going to change my ways.' Would you accept this?

There would be a lot of people who wouldn't. They'd say, 'You've made your bed and now you have to lie in it.' In the past I may have reacted similarly, but today I don't feel that way. I don't want to punish someone for mistakes or assume that because they thought one way for a long time, they can't have an epiphany. We are all capable of growth and change.

Every conversation is different. But if I do decide to speak up with the aim of changing someone's mind, I tend to do the following . . .

- **Bring it back to a human level.** I find it's really useful to remind people that when they say things in broad strokes about a certain group of people they're talking about humans with real lives. Ask them what their friends might think about their opinion. Or ask them to think about if what they're saying might be harmful towards an individual or group. Bringing it all back to human experience can help remind someone who they could be hurting with their words.
- **Remind them that this isn't an attack.** It's helpful to remind people that having a difference of opinion isn't a personal attack. Regulate your tone to ensure that they recognize this and to show that you're approaching the conversation in a calm way. This is particularly

important if we're talking over text messages or social media. I tend to begin with something along the lines of, 'This is said with love,' or 'Please don't read this in an angry tone – that's not my intention.'

- **Remember that we're all on different timelines.** Just because someone has a different opinion to you doesn't make them a terrible person. Some people reach a state of understanding with issues faster than others. We should all be giving each other grace and time to process information. Sometimes I may say something, and it might not land straight away. But that doesn't mean that person might not consider and take on board my point at a later date.

- **Think about language.** There are already so many potential barriers and obstacles to these tricky discussions and using overcomplicated language or words that aren't commonly known doesn't help – in fact, it can just alienate people, as they could see the issues you're raising as things that don't apply to them. I try to make sure not to intellectualize too much in terms of the language that I use, and I break down points in ways everyone can understand. Someone shouldn't need a dictionary to be able to understand your points, nor should they have to have read every book you have – you should be able to explain yourself in a way that the majority of people will understand.

- **Ask questions.** I find this a really useful way to neutralize a situation, or to try to get to the bottom of why someone thinks the way they do. I'll ask, 'Where

did you learn this?' or 'Why do you think this way?'
I've found that the smartest people are often the ones
who ask questions. Also, if someone is using language
you don't understand, you shouldn't be afraid to ask
for more clarification – knowledge is power. You could
say, 'Can you break that down in more simple terms
for me?' or 'I don't understand what you mean by
that – can you clarify?' If they can't, then they probably
don't understand their topic as well as they initially
made out.

You tried your best!

During each conversation, I'm trying to recognize if
someone is taking my points on board and if they're
granting me the same empathy I am granting them. I ask
myself, '*Do they seem receptive to my points? Are they
listening, or are they interrupting me and doubling down
on their original point?*' If I feel like I am getting nowhere,
I decide to step away.

Unfortunately not everyone will listen or grant you
empathy and patience. Some people will stubbornly refuse
to acknowledge what you are saying. Then there are those
who have been told time and time again that what they're
doing causes harm, but *still* carry on. There *are* instances
when it's just not worth your time. If you feel like you're
getting nowhere, the person you're talking to is a drain on
your energy or the language they are using is incredibly
violent and hurtful, then you can leave the conversation.

It's not your job to change every single individual's mind. Save yourself for the moments when you can.

There are a few people in my life with whom we've exhausted a topic to such an extent that we have reached a state of disagreement – we have simply recognized that we can't change each other's minds. For example, I have a few friends who refuse to engage with politics at all. I've tried to explain to them that if you don't do politics, politics will do you, but for a huge number of reasons, some just refuse to engage. As frustrating as it is, you can't force people to believe things.

In these scenarios, I've learned that it's best to just exercise acceptance. I know that I've put my point across well, but ultimately I can't change people. Often – particularly with some really tough issues, such as those regarding politics – not everyone has the capacity, headspace or the will, and just because they aren't engaging now doesn't mean they won't in the future. They may come back to these issues in their own time.

There are many reasons why someone may not be as receptive to listening to you as you would like. I discuss this in further detail later in this chapter, but an important element of having good conversations is also being able to recognize that often people have views due to their past. While this doesn't mean we have to agree with them, we do have to have empathy that they're approaching and viewing issues from a completely different place from us. For example, someone may have been raised with misogynistic views on women because of how they saw their father or other male figures speak or behave around women. It's important for them to make efforts to change, but it's also important for us to be understanding about the fact that the way they've been raised to view the world is entirely different from our own, and that is not their fault.

Feeling all the feels

Sometimes it can seem like the best thing to be in a conversation is numb. When people get passionate about subjects they care deeply about, they might get told to 'stop being dramatic' or told to 'calm down'. It can seem like our feelings and emotions may be held against us, and that if we raise our voices or burst into tears during a tough conversation, we've failed. But feeling emotional – particularly when talking about really heavy, often personal, subjects – is natural. And you shouldn't be afraid to show that you care. It's more than likely that during some conversations a whole host of emotions will come up: anger, sadness, frustration. It's unfair that our emotions are ever used against us, but they so often are.

There will be times when emotions get the better of you. This can happen in the conversations you've prepared for and the conversations you haven't. Again, I've learned over time that you can master your emotions and use them to drive you and your cause further forward.

Anger can be a very effective tool for me. My drive is often at its most powerful when I'm angry about something.

I wish it wasn't this way – that it was enough for someone like me to live their life proudly and happily without needing to be angry or have something to fight against. But then something will happen in the world and I'm pulled back down to earth. But I recognize that every time I get angry and I use it to be vocal about what's really happening, I'm fighting for myself and for others like me to be happy.

When I've spoken up in the past about the oppression that I see all around me, or how our society still operates under a system of white supremacy, it's always been anger that has driven me to do so. Events unfolded that I felt I had to speak out on, and I would recognize that I'm not the only one who felt this way. Each time I speak out, I'm aware that my community will be feeling the same hurt, anger and disappointment, and that they are backing me.

Anger is an incredible tool. You can harness it in a way that brings about positive change, but you have to manage it carefully and make sure – and this applies to any emotion that drives you – that it doesn't become you.

In the UK in 2024, there was a general election when the country was able to vote in a new political party. For so long in the UK, the Conservative Party had been in power and there was this sense of 'Tories out' at any cost. Keir Starmer (Labour's leader and, at the time of writing, the UK's prime minister) had made comments that much of the transgender community found offensive and concerning,[16] and yet many left-leaning people were still planning on voting for him. I found myself getting more and more frustrated at people thinking that trans rights were an acceptable sacrifice. I could have viewed it as a personal attack, as the things Keir Starmer was saying were so close to home. Instead, during discussions I tried to direct this anger into pointing out to people how the electoral system worked and encouraging them to do research into voting within their area. Polls showed that Labour were going to win by a landslide, so I asked people whether they felt their vote for Labour really was needed to 'get the Tories out' or if they could vote for another party to help increase its parliamentary seats.

So often news stories that I see in the media anger me. But before I react immediately, I try to take some time to assess my anger and analyse where it's rooted. I take a step back and find some space to examine where my anger has come from and what I am going to do with it. I say again and again that we shouldn't just feel our emotions, but instead examine them. This is a skill that takes time to develop, but it will ultimately help you to know yourself so much better, including knowing when to use your emotions as a driving force and when to pull them back.

It's incredibly difficult in a moment of rage to understand why you're feeling angry. But here are some questions I will often ask myself when I see something in the news or on social media, or hear something in a conversation that riles me up:

- **What is it about this story or conversation that has made me so angry?** When it came to the election and I saw people posting about voting for Labour, I could root that back to Keir Starmer's comments and how I saw this as a dismissal of my and my communities' rights. I could see I wasn't directly angry at the people themselves but more the wider issue at play that trans lives are so often used as pawns within political discussions without thinking of the people directly impacted.
- **What else is happening in my life right now?** Sometimes I can find myself getting more angry than usual about a situation, and that is often down to something else that's going on. If there are personal issues that could be impacting my reactions, I try to deal with those first, as otherwise I'm more likely to explode with anger and say something I might regret.
- **How can I channel my anger?** So much of activism is fuelled by anger, but we have to funnel it in the right way. This could be collectively – like going to a protest and being with others who feel the same pain and anger as me – or it could be figuring out what I could do that would actually make a difference. I couldn't tell people

how to vote or be personally annoyed at them, but I could try something more practical, like reminding them to look into certain political policies and the systems in place.

If you find your anger is rising in a conversation, and you feel that the person you're speaking to isn't intentionally making you angry, there could still be space for a useful, positive discussion. You could use your anger to direct the discussion into a more helpful place. Say you've recognized that you're angry because a conversation sparked something personal – it could be helpful to move on from your own feelings and experiences into a wider topic. It's an opportunity to say, 'We shouldn't be talking about personal, individual situations but instead talking about the system.'

For example, I've had frustrating conversations where I've been speaking out against the treatment of Black and trans people in the UK, and I've been asked how I can complain when I have gained success as a Black trans woman myself. They use me as a signal to point to things getting better. It's as if they're saying because I've been on the cover of British *Vogue*, that means things are OK.

That makes me angry. It's a clear example of someone using my personal individual circumstances to make a point about the wider world. I want to be using my platform and influence as a role model in the right way, but my individual circumstances are not indicative of what is happening around me. I take that frustration, and

I use it to drive my argument – to remind people that I am the exception to the rule. Just because I am on the cover of a magazine doesn't change the statistics that show how trans people are more likely to experience homelessness, or that trans kids are self-harming at an exponential rate, or that powerful people across the world are winding back access to trans healthcare. I bring it back to the political.

Of course, not everything that sparks anger is personal. As empathetic human beings we will get upset and angry at the injustice we see in the world, even when it doesn't impact us directly.

And it is *so* natural to feel angry. When I discuss learning how to channel anger, I do not mean that we should be suppressing it. I've found that I am often praised for 'not rising' and 'not shouting' when I'm placed in situations opposite people who disagree with me. And so often in these scenarios, it's not just that these people are disagreeing with my viewpoints – they're actually debating my entire existence. Often, people say things to me – like during the debate regarding the gender on my passport that I mentioned earlier – that I would be well within my rights to be angry about.

And I should be *allowed* to get angry. But our passion, as minority groups, is often used against us. It suggests that the violence is coming from those that want the change rather than the people who are oppressing them. Even by praising me for remaining calm, it's suggesting that people shouldn't stand up for their beliefs in an impassioned way. The idea that our anger invalidates our argument when we are simply expressing ourselves about the injustice that we have faced is deeply unfair. This is a conversation we still need to have.

Why do so many people feel that righteous rage is wrong? Why do we expect those who have experienced violence to speak about things in a measured and digestible way? Why do we assume that emotions invalidate arguments?

Women shouldn't have to be polite about misogyny.
Black people shouldn't have to be jolly about racism.

Trans people shouldn't have to be calm about transphobia. Gay people shouldn't have to be stoic in the face of homophobia. These are all things to be angry about.

But we do have to look into *how* we use that anger – ensuring that we use it in a way that brings about real change, by funnelling it into something else, rather than allowing those feelings to stay inside and fester. We do that by our actions and by keeping going, even when we want to give up or just scream.

When to step away

Yes, it's important that we have these conversations. It's important to speak up about things that matter to you; to speak to friends when they say harmful things; to discuss issues with family; and to use your voice to highlight the causes you care about. But it's also so important to know when you're not ready to have these conversations.

Recognizing when you're ready to speak up and when is the right time to do so is something that – with time – you'll learn. If one person in the conversation isn't ready – or you both aren't – things can really escalate. It's important to learn how to distinguish between a helpful, enlightening conversation, and an argument. In a conversation, we converse. In an argument, we're often shouting. Or if we're not shouting, we feel terse and tense. We're certainly not listening to each other. Sometimes we end up in conversations where we are simply going round and round in circles, growing more and more frustrated as it seems nothing is sinking in. It's a place of unease, upset, and where no one is taking anything on board.

Ask yourself:

- How well do I know what I want to say, and how I want to say it?
- Do I think this person is going to be receptive to what I'm saying?
- Is this person willing to listen to me and to see my side?
- How receptive do I feel to what they're saying?
- How vulnerable do I feel today?
- Are we really going to learn from each other in this moment of time?
- Is this going to bring about change?
- Is this going to hurt or dishearten me?
- Will this be a drain on my energy and time?

Each and every conversation you have is different. You could have had a conversation with the same person at another time and in a different place that went well but find that this time it doesn't feel that way. I know when I am feeling too raw for discussions, or when I find myself getting upset by things that don't normally bother me, such as nasty comments on my Instagram or in my DMs. Normally I brush them off and think, '*It's just someone hurt and angry with themselves.*' But there are days when the comments sting, and I know that for me, it probably isn't the best time to actively engage in tough conversations. Instead I will wait until my energy is restored and I feel more balanced.

I have also started to turn down television 'debates', as so often the person I am being invited to speak with is anti-trans. It's presented as being in the interest of balance, but so often, that person is not willing to listen. I spoke earlier about what makes a good conversation, and it has to be a meeting of minds – not just bashing heads. I also think there are some things that are just not up for debate. You wouldn't in good faith invite a Black person to debate with a white supremacist, or a Jewish person to debate with an anti-Semite, or a woman to debate with a violent misogynist or an incel – yet I'm regularly invited to debate my reality as a transgender person with people who deny it. People who aren't even willing to listen.

You can often spot these sorts of scenarios when someone is just repeating their point over and over, or pushing the conversation into a place where they're deliberately trying to goad you by bringing in personal experience. They're not asking you for your opinion so they can learn; they are asking you to speak so that they can then speak over you and push their agenda.

This is not to say you should never converse with someone who disagrees with you. There are so many different elements at play that can make a conversation incredibly difficult, but these same elements can also be the reason to have that discussion. It could be that they're in your family, and you love them, but you need them to hear your perspective. Or because you're in a relationship and you worry for the future of that relationship. Or because they're your friend and you don't want to hurt them. So many conversations are hard to have and so many *are* worth it in the end. But they'll only be worth it if you're *all* in the right headspace to talk. Assess that and go from there.

If you decide it's not going to be worth it or that the conversation could easily tip into an argument, then it's perfectly OK to step away and wait until circumstances are different and you feel ready. Take some time to weigh up how much you want to have the particular conversation and how much it will be worth it in the long run.

For real change to happen we have to ensure our words are reaching those who are listening and who will treat them with respect. If we don't feel that is the case, then it is our right to disengage and step away.

Another thing to consider is whether this is a topic you actually want to be discussing. I know that there are traumatic moments in my past that can cause me to spiral. I have, over the years, recognized that conversations surrounding sexual assault can trigger a lot for me personally and will often destabilize me. I stand in solidarity with survivors, but I find it difficult to hear other people's experiences, as they will trigger me into recalling the details of my own assault.

These conversations absolutely should be happening, but I know I will not always be able to give them the energy and focus that's required. It's important to remember that you're not beholden to anybody. Nowadays I am very upfront, and if I recognize that a conversation will drain or trigger me, I'll either not enter into it at all, or I'll say something like, 'I'm sorry, I can't participate in this right now – it's just too close to home,' or, 'I can recognize that, at this moment, this conversation will not be good for my mental health.' Then I'll completely disengage.

Learn how to preserve your power and your peace.

Let's talk about talking online

The online world used to be the main platform for my cause. I was very active online, but eventually, I began to feel burned out from all the pressure to comment on every single thing that was going on. This came mostly from a sense of personal responsibility: I was a trans person with a platform, and I felt like if I didn't use that and speak out as a voice for other marginalized people then it was a wasted opportunity.

There had been a number of high-profile attacks and murders in my community at the time when my online platform was growing, and I couldn't sit by and watch the world causing so much pain for trans people. I believed that because I was in a position where I could educate others on these issues then I had to, each and every time I saw an opportunity to do so. However, ultimately it not only left me open to attacks and trolling, but it wasn't having the impact I wanted it to.

I began to realize that the conversations I was having online weren't really conversations at all. They were less about listening to one another and often became quite personal because the element of humanity had been taken out. We don't see each other as real online as we are hidden behind screens, whereas having conversations in person tends to bring out a greater level of respect as it's harder to ignore the other person's humanity.

Now I'm so much less active on social media. I never enter into 'debates' in the comment section. I only speak on things publicly when I feel confident, stable and educated enough to do so. I also often find it helpful to use my online platform to highlight the work that other people are doing. It's not that I don't think that speaking out on social media is important – it is. But being an online activist can take its toll, and I wanted to find more ways to take my activism offline.

If you are like me – someone who likes to speak up against injustice – then holding back from speaking up each and every time you see something wrong can be a tough adjustment. But it would be impossible to know or learn everything about, or comment on, all the injustice. There's an infinite number of things wrong with the world. Recognizing this not only helps us avoid performative activism (see page 40), but also stops us from getting burned out. Remember, you are just one cog in the activism machine, and you cannot fix everything.

Today I've learned to find balance with my online and offline activism. When I get an inkling that I might be pushing myself too far, I take a moment and begin pulling back. When you don't think you are the right person to be speaking about something online, but you want to support a cause, think about what else you can be doing offline.

Perhaps you could take to the streets and join a protest or community action? There's energy to be found in being around other people who feel the same way as you. Plus it stops you feeling that immense pressure to do it all, as you realize how many other people are supporting a cause.

Or perhaps you could read up on the issue? As you know, gaining knowledge is powerful and it is still a form of action. You can feel quietly confident that you are taking strides forward without rushing to take action in a way that may not be entirely helpful.

When everyone seems to be posting about a particular issue, it's understandable to want to get involved. But real and authentic activism is about ignoring that pressure and carving out an identity for yourself that is true and authentic to you. And you don't need an online presence at all – there are plenty of activists who don't. Pay attention to your feelings and be honest with yourself. How does social media make you feel? Find what works for you, and you might discover that the reward will come not from likes or shares, but from stepping out into the world and having real conversations.

Talking to family (and friends who feel like family)

When we love someone and our lives are woven together, challenging one another or disagreeing over an issue can be tough. I've always found the conversations with the people that I'm closest to are a lot harder than those with strangers. Preparing for those conversations and having discussions with your family and friends is completely different from giving a speech or having a debate with either a peer or someone you don't know so well. Your family or childhood friends are the people who have known you the longest in the whole world, and as a result the conversations can be really emotionally turbulent.

With family, you could find yourself being infantilized, dismissed or even punished. And while friendships can be uplifting and beautiful, they aren't always easy, and you can feel let down by friends when they hold opinions that don't align with your own. People change over time as well. We have to allow people to evolve and grow, but with that change a void can appear – where once-close relationships no longer feel as treasured and special as they once were.

I've lost friends through having some really tough conversations. Today I can recognize that this isn't necessarily a bad thing. We shouldn't be friends with people who make us feel bad or who uphold values that impact our very existence in a negative way. Up until 2020 and the conversations surrounding the Black Lives Matter movement, I would make allowances for people and avoid difficult conversations with them. But then when it became the right time to have those conversations, some friends were absolutely unwilling to have them.

That's not to say that by raising and discussing tough topics with your friends and family the outcome is always going to be a negative one. I've had so many life-affirming conversations where my friends have buoyed me and reminded me of my power. I've also had conversations with friends where, at the end, we've reached a state of neutrality and decided that we will neither agree nor disagree on a topic. There are also people who I simply don't discuss the tough subjects with. There once was a time I thought I should only be friends with people who were politically active and engaged, but now I've come to realize there are many reasons why someone may want to back out of a conversation or not engage with a topic, and it doesn't mean that they don't care. We're all different people muddling along through life, trying to do the very best we can with what we've been given. It's this empathy that I grant everyone, and I expect the same back.

It's trickier with family as often we can feel incredibly tied to them. Plus from my experience, no one can make you as angry as your own family! Regulating emotions with your relatives can be a lot trickier. We can also feel with our family (and to some extent our close friends) that it's our job to change their minds. But it's not, particularly if doing so is going to put you or anyone else in a place that's unsafe – and safety can mean many things. It's not just about feeling physically safe, but emotionally too.

The first step before embarking on a conversation with a loved one is self-reflection . . .

Step one: Talking to yourself

You *need* to be on your own side. You need to protect your energy. Make sure that you're in the mindset to have a conversation and not an argument. As we discussed earlier, mental preparation before any big conversation is vital, but even more so when it comes to speaking with the people that we love as emotions are always going to be heightened and we will feel things more deeply. Ask yourself the questions we explored earlier, such as, '*How do I feel today? Why do I feel this way? What have I absorbed this week that could be impacting how I normally respond?*' This is a good practice to get into regularly, not just in the moments leading up to a conversation.

We shouldn't be afraid to ask ourselves these questions. It's so easy to think that every problem that we face is external but sometimes the issue is internal. Our feelings are so often indicators of something larger going on in our lives.

I've found that the more you get to know yourself, the easier it is to enforce boundaries and know if it's the right time to be entering into a conversation. You'll begin to recognize what your limits are as you notice the patterns of your own behaviour. Conversations with loved ones can feel even more personal and emotional than others, so check in with yourself and make sure you're ready for it.

Step two: Understanding them

You know that when *you're* tired and snappy you won't be in the best mental state to have a tough conversation. Well, this also applies to the loved one you're speaking to. Before raising anything, have a think about how they're behaving. Do they seem argumentative? Are they being snappy? If you don't feel like either of you are in a good place to have a helpful discussion, then it's perfectly OK to draw a boundary and step away. Then you could simply file it away as something to be raised another day, knowing that the conversation is necessary but that today isn't the right time to do it.

Or if during the discussion you begin to notice their energy levels are dropping or they're becoming snappy, you can use similar phrases to those we discussed when we spoke about protecting yourself, and simply say, 'I want this conversation to come from a place of love. To ensure we're both in the right headspace, shall we park it for now?' That way the conversation can still happen in the future, when you're both in a better position to have it.

Whenever the conversation takes place, it's vital that you enter into it with empathy. It sounds strange to say this about a friend or relative, but you have to get to know each other first! You need to try and figure out if you have a difference of opinion (which you may not – sometimes people surprise you) and, if you do, where that difference lies. This is an opportunity to get to know them, how they grew up and how their opinion was formed. Particularly with family, when there are generational differences at play, you can begin to understand them so much more – and be able to communicate better – if you can examine how they grew up and what that time period was like for them. Opinions are so often formed through personal experience, so can you uncover why they might feel the way that they feel?

My experiences growing up gay under Section 28 were by no means as brutal and violent as the experiences of those growing up in the 1980s during the HIV/AIDS epidemic, when hundreds of thousands of people died across the world from the illness. The gay community were being unfairly blamed for the disease and the stigma was so great that they were being evicted from their homes and kept segregated in hospitals. People debated on television whether gay people should be quarantined. Instead of researching for a treatment for the illness, the media and the government demonized and blamed a marginalized community, putting them at further risk. The mental health impact of that time is still very much felt today. Similarly, I know that the lived experience of those who grew up gay in the 1940s and 1950s – when being openly gay was illegal – will have had a long-lasting effect on how comfortable they feel speaking about certain topics.

We need to listen to and honour and understand each other's histories, as every single generation has had different experiences, traumas and difficulties. We can often take for granted the things we have today. Take mental health support – if someone is being hugely dismissive of our need for it, it could be an emotional reaction due to their own past and how they felt the need to bottle up their feelings under societal or family pressure. It could be difficult for them to acknowledge that there was another way they could have lived – one that perhaps would have caused them less pain. This way of thinking doesn't just apply to those older than us, but also those our own age who may have been raised with different values instilled in them, or pressure from their own families to behave in a certain way.

But if you're honouring that, then you deserve the same treatment from them. They should listen to you speak of your experiences and how you feel. For example, a lot of young people experienced the COVID-19 pandemic and lockdown in a completely different way from the older generations. If you were in good health, then you were considered of lower priority at the beginning stages of the pandemic than those who were older or who had underlying health conditions.

And while the threat to your physical health didn't loom as large, over time, the isolation, the disruption to school or university life, and the impact on future prospects could all have had a big effect on your mental health. If one person spent their lockdown in a large home with a garden then they may not have found the time so bad compared to someone else who was cut off from friends and living in cramped living spaces or having to share a bedroom. See how people can go through the same thing, but have totally different experiences? It's important that both people in a conversation are willing to acknowledge that and give time to truly listen to what the other has to say.

Uncovering the place someone is coming from may take time. It may take more than one conversation. It's about asking questions like, 'Where did this opinion come from? Can you remember when you first learned that?'

With friends, this might be a little easier than with family, as ultimately you can choose your friends, but you can't choose your biological family. This means you may end up in situations where you're speaking to relatives with incredibly different views from you that, normally, you'd want to step away from.

Please always remember that no matter what your relationship is with someone, if a conversation is moving to an aggressive place, or in a violent or bigoted direction, you can remove yourself from it. You have the right to advocate for yourself. No one should be offended by you setting a boundary. You don't have to be beholden to someone just because they share your DNA or they've played a huge part in your history.

Step three: Make sure the conversation is going places

If you are experiencing a disagreement with a friend or family member, in order to be able to move forward with your relationship you need to decide what you want from the conversation.

You need to be able to assess what you want the outcome to be and whether realistically you are going to get it. If you're not going to get the person to come round to your way of thinking, how does that make you feel? Are you willing to acknowledge that there might be a scenario where you're both right? Or that you could be wrong? Or that they are wrong, but it isn't coming from a bad or hateful place and so it feels OK? We will cover this more in the next chapter, but when talking with friends and family, you really have to consider what the relationship means to you and how their views on a certain topic impact you.

If I am in a conversation with someone close to me who seems open to my point of view, willing to see where they might be wrong, and respectful of other people's experiences, sometimes that can be enough – even if ultimately you have different opinions.

However, as I've done so much inner work on myself and how to recognize my boundaries in order to protect my energy, I have also come to realize that not all friendships need clinging on to at all costs. I've taken this realization into mind with every tough conversation that I've had with friends.

If I have a different viewpoint from a friend, I want us to be examining that. Sometimes our views are so different that friendship just isn't possible. If someone's views are rooted in a refusal to see the humanity in people then that is something I am not willing to accept. If someone is not willing to explore further with you why they think the way they think, then depending on how that makes you feel, you may need to let them go.

Talking points

Every conversation you have is going to be different. Even when we think we know exactly how the conversation will go because we are talking to the people we love most in the world and who we know inside out . . . a curveball could be thrown, veering the conversation off course.

Whether you're talking with strangers on a wider platform or with your friends and family, discussing the big issues can be scary. The more you do it, the more you learn how to handle even the trickiest of moments. You also learn just how powerful these conversations can be for both you and the people that you're speaking with. That these conversations are worth having, but only on the occasions when it feels right for both of you.

Remember . . .

- **Conversations don't always happen on a schedule.** There are some conversations that you can prepare for . . . and some that will be sprung on you. The more you know your subject and prepare *when you can*, the easier you'll find any moments when preparation isn't possible.
- **It's OK to step away. At any point.** You don't owe anyone anything and it's not your job to change people's minds – even those closest to you. Their opinions do not reflect on yours and it can be freeing to just allow people to think how they think and know that you won't ever agree.
- **Emotions can be powerful.** Our passion is so often used against us but it's our passion that keeps driving us forward, so watch out for people who want to use your anger against you.
- **Take it offline.** I believe the best conversations happen in person, when we can see each other's humanity. There

are so many ways to get your voice and opinions across that don't involve social media.

- **Conversations with friends and family can be the toughest of all.** Make sure you're all ready before entering into them.

4

We Need to Talk About... Being Wrong

How do you feel when you get something wrong? I don't mean when you fail a test or confuse one thing for another, but instead when you've held an opinion – perhaps really strongly – and then someone points out to you that it's not rooted in fact, or that it's not taking into account the experiences of someone else. It can be an awful feeling! We may have hurt someone by clumsily throwing our opinion in without having properly researched why we think that way or considered those directly impacted. Or we could just be a little embarrassed and feel that horrible dread in our stomach that arrives with shame.

But what if I told you that you *have* to be wrong to ever be right? That not only is it OK if you mess things up, but actually it's a vital part of your life journey? Today, I feel so content in who I am and what I stand for, but I couldn't have reached this stage of my life by getting it right all the time because I wouldn't have learned anything. There have been *so* many times where I've got things wrong, but I have taken each of those moments as an opportunity to grow and allow myself to change.

Uncomfortable moments lead to personal growth.

Something I've learned is that we shouldn't talk about right and wrong in such absolute terms. When we're having conversations about issues that impact people and our world, there will be complexities and nuance to them. It's almost impossible to do the right thing *all the time*. Take cars and planes – we know that they're causing harm to our environment, yet so many of us use them. We can care deeply about the environment and still be doing things that damage it.

We're also expanding our knowledge and learning new information all the time about this world and the people in it. There are so many phrases and words that were once commonly used, but when people began speaking out against them and pointing out that they were harmful to certain communities, we stopped. Just because something was OK at one point in time, doesn't mean it will remain that way forever. Things can change. And with all these changes happening, it's perfectly normal to get things wrong sometimes.

All we can do is enter conversations with an open mind and be willing to learn from our mistakes. Remember . . .

- What you thought was correct may not be.
- You could be right, and the other person could *also* be right.
- What you know may not be the full picture, as everyone has a fresh perspective to bring to a topic.
- Two or more things can be true at once. You may have lived through something and had a particular experience of it, while another person could have lived through that *exact* same experience and felt very differently.

Throughout your activism and this journey you're going to get things wrong. This isn't always a bad thing, and when you reframe the idea of 'being wrong' to see it as an opportunity for growth, it makes the thought of it a lot less scary. It can also improve your discussions. How? If you're going in knowing that you could be wrong and owning that possibility, then you'll be more engaged in the conversation and what the other person is saying, as you won't be focusing too much on not making any mistakes.

'Mistakes' are just another step on your activism journey.

That's not to say you should just bulldoze into any conversation without fully understanding the issue – particularly if your words could end up causing hurt. Just because we learn from being wrong doesn't mean we should *aim* to be wrong. There are effective ways that we will be going over in more detail in this chapter that can help us limit how often we're wrong while also helping us gain a greater understanding of ourselves and those around us. They include harnessing your listening skills, passing the mic, knowing how and when to apologize and allowing others the space to be wrong, and they are all tricky things to navigate, as they involve approaching each situation differently and being able to recognize the nuance within people and their lives. So, let's talk about getting it wrong and what we can do about it . . .

Being innocently wrong

I've seen it happen so many times that when people are trying too hard to be right, they get it totally wrong instead. These are people who have the absolute best intentions at heart but have just blundered in, thinking they know the solution and how to help without the necessary research.

We spoke in Chapter 2 about the importance of allies and how we all have to come together to reach a better future. To do that, I encouraged you to use your imagination and initiative to think of solutions. But be careful, as from my experience people often get things wrong in activist spaces when they *want* to do the right thing, but they don't consult the right people. Or if they do speak to the right people, they don't properly listen to what they say. Then there are those who want to take the reins themselves when in reality they would be better off playing a more backstage role and supporting other voices.

In 2023 I was asked to be involved in a protest speaking out against the UK government's decisions regarding trans rights, as it had announced that it intended to ban trans people from single-sex wards in hospitals.[17] To protest this and showcase solidarity, a cisgender person wanted to arrange a rally outside Downing Street. The problem was that they went ahead and began organizing the protest in partnership with the local police force.

That very same year, the Metropolitan Police (who serve the Greater London area) had been found to be institutionally racist, misogynistic and homophobic in a report carried out by Louise Casey.[18] This report was commissioned in the wake of the abduction, rape and murder of Sarah Everard by serving Metropolitan Police officer Wayne Couzens. These findings came as no surprise to the communities that this directly impacts and mean that at the very roots of the police force there are deeply harmful practices that impact marginalized people.

The trans experience wasn't part of the report, but most people within the trans community will tell you that we don't have a good relationship with the police. A 2020 report by Dr Cerys Bradley for the LGBTQIA+ anti-abuse charity Galop found that just 1 in 7 transgender people in the UK are likely to report a transphobic incident to the police.[19] It also found that more than 1 in 3 respondents who chose not to report did so because they were fearful of transphobia from the police force, and 7 in 10 respondents felt that the police could not help them.

Unfortunately this isn't only the case in the UK. In America it's been found that trans people are 3.7 times more likely to experience police violence than cis people.[20] And that's not taking into account that often when we experience violence or an attack – particularly at the hands of those who hold power – we may not report it. If the person organizing the protest had consulted trans people *before* arranging it, then they would have heard all sorts of stories of blatant discrimination from police officers. But they didn't.

When the organizer shared their plans on social media, the protest didn't land well. I declined to take part (sharing my feelings privately instead), but it was a clear example of how someone wanted to do something good but then formed their solution too quickly and without a proper understanding of the issues faced by the community they were trying to help.

It's completely understandable – particularly in our fast-paced news culture – that we want to rush to come up with solutions and show our solidarity to those who need it. But remember, change doesn't happen overnight, and it is far more effective to slow down and take your time to figure out what would be the best course of action.

It's really important to constantly remind yourself that all the injustices that you see playing out on the news or on your social media feeds are happening to human beings. Each news story has a real-world impact and often affects a huge number of people. So, if you want to help the people at the heart of those stories, you need to consider . . .

- how much you have read up on this situation. As we covered in Chapter 1, you need to read widely on a topic and ensure that you're listening to those directly impacted. This may involve looking beyond mainstream media and seeing what people are saying on social media or in their individually produced newsletters. Then ask yourself, 'How can I help those people? What would they like me to do?'
- whether the people affected by this issue are working with any organizations that you could reach out to and offer support, or if they have organized a march that you could join.
- the needs of the community itself. If you have your own ideas that you think could help, then it's important to – after doing your own research – consult someone in that community and ask them what they think. Is your idea something that will help them? Or would they prefer you used your energy elsewhere?

With the trans rights protest, it all could have gone very differently had the person in question done any of the above when organizing. Yes, they came to the community impacted to involve us in their protest, but only after they'd already gone ahead and begun to shout about it on social media. What they could have done instead was come to someone they knew in the community who they trusted or approached one of the leading organizations and said, 'I'd love to help with this and show my support. I had this idea . . . what do you think?' or instead asked, 'Are there any ongoing campaigns that I could lend my platform and my voice to?'

One of the biggest things we will be discussing in this chapter is how to recognize where your voice is best used. None of us know all the answers, particularly when we're talking about experiences that don't impact us directly.

You and your voice hold so much power – you just need to make sure you're using it in the best and most sensitive way . . .

Have you checked your privilege?

Have you ever had a first-aid lesson and learned how to give CPR? Did you notice that the mannequins used to teach us how to give this life-saving exercise are always men? Or that plasters – until very recently – were only available in a white skin tone? These are just two examples of how our society is built in a way that prioritizes white cisgender men. It also doesn't just come down to how products are designed but also the ways in which men can exist: they can be assertive without being labelled 'bossy', or they can walk down the street at night without feeling afraid of being attacked. There are so many ways in which men hold privilege in society.

In Chapter 1, I spoke about intersectional feminism – and this is acknowledging that while white men hold privilege over women, white women will still hold privilege over women of colour. This shows itself in many ways – again in both the products available to us and the ways we exist in the world. It includes the lack of foundations in a diverse range of skin tones and how, when styled naturally, Afro hair has been found to be viewed as 'messy' and 'unprofessional' in the workplace.[21] We also are given fewer opportunities and have to face racism and discrimination in many areas of our lives.

So, what do people mean when they say 'check your privilege'? It is all about being able to acknowledge that your day-to-day experiences may be easier because of your gender, race, class, sexuality or whether or not you're able-bodied. In other words, being a white, straight, able-bodied man awards you many privileges that make your life easier. Or how being a white, straight, able-bodied woman can still make your life considerably easier than those of women of colour or those who have disabilities.

I've noticed that people will often apologize for their privilege, and I don't necessarily think that it's something that anyone needs to apologize for. But you should understand how you can utilize your privilege to help and raise others up. For example, no one is expecting white people to apologize for being white. But it's important for white people to understand that their whiteness allows them to move through the world feeling safer, more protected and listened to – and to then think about how they can use this to help others.

Privilege itself isn't a problem if you're using it in the right way.

There are privileges within marginalized communities as well. I'm aware that as a mixed-race, light-skinned Black woman, I'm not experiencing the same level of hardship and discrimination within society than if I was a dark-skinned

Black woman. This is largely because my facial features and skin tone are more aligned with the Eurocentric societal 'ideal' of what is considered to be beautiful. Colourism, like racism, has a deep-rooted history that goes all the way back to when enslaved people with lighter complexions were allowed to perform less strenuous tasks, such as domestic duties, while darker-skinned enslaved people were forced to engage in hard labour, usually out in the fields.

Discrimination and privilege have been part of our society for centuries, and the current structures we live under have been built upon them. It's up to those who hold privilege to acknowledge this, learn about how discrimination manifests, and think about how they could even out the playing field.

Those who experience oppression don't always have the words or examples to explain something that is so pervasive and woven into our society. You have to listen and believe them when they discuss their experiences navigating a world that has been designed for those who are not like them.

A really powerful way to utilize your privilege for good is by recognizing when you should take the lead and when you should be allowing others to speak instead.

Everyone should have the freedom to tell their own stories.

Let me explain that for you . . .

Perhaps you are someone who always likes to speak up and say what needs to be said. However, we must allow people to speak on the issues that directly impact them. Have you ever heard someone being accused of mansplaining? 'Mansplaining' is when a man tries to explain something to a woman who already understands the topic – often in a patronizing way. For example, when a man tries to explain an issue that women face . . . to a woman. It might come from a good place of showing understanding and compassion, but speaking over someone and not allowing them to share their own lived experience because they feel they already know better is not a helpful way to have a conversation.

But it's not only men who do this. It can be done by anyone – you and I included! I am particularly conscious of doing this if I'm part of a conversation about the experience of a racial group I am not part of, or when there's conversations around disability or neurodivergence. That's not to say I won't lend my opinion or voice to issues surrounding disabled people, but there's a very fine line between speaking about a topic and speaking over those who have more knowledge and authority on a subject.

So how do you find that balance? Whether it's in your activism or your personal life, you need to consciously consider the following:

● **Who are you speaking to?** Whatever situation you're in, you should be thinking about who you're with and what they could bring to the conversation.

- **Are you being curious and asking questions?** You shouldn't make assumptions about anyone, and it's always better to ask them questions about their own personal experiences.
- **Has your ego taken over?** Your focus shouldn't be on making yourself look good – it should be on learning, absorbing and trying to understand.
- **Are you allowing others to speak?** If you know that someone has lived experience, are they being given the opportunity to share that, or are you talking over someone who has more knowledge on a matter? It might not even be intentional – you might be someone who is confident, or someone that people naturally gravitate towards. Use this privilege to direct the conversation towards someone else. You can say, 'I'd love to hear what you have to say on the matter – what do you think?'
- **What are other people in the room doing?** Be observant. Have you noticed that someone who has something to say is being silenced or talked over? Can you bring them into the discussion? Give them space to talk by being quiet and truly listening. This is what's known as 'passing the mic'.

Passing the mic

One of the ways I've been trying to pass the mic in my own life is by spotlighting and amplifying the voices of transgender children.

In June 2024, a group of teenagers scaled an NHS building in London and camped out on the building's ledge. Their signs read 'we are not pawns for your politics' and 'Trans Kids Deserve Better' (which was the name of the network they belonged to).[22] The protest came in the wake of the government restricting access to all puberty blockers in the UK. This is an incredibly dangerous move and goes against the advice of the trans community, and LGBTQIA+ charities like Stonewall fear it will 'cause stress and uncertainty for many trans youth'.[23]

It shouldn't be this way. These teenagers shouldn't have to fight for access to vital healthcare. It's understandable that some activists want to speak on behalf of them, but I saw this as a real opportunity for older, more experienced activists to pass the mic to those who are directly impacted by this decision. This felt particularly important as one of the arguments against puberty blockers is that queer youth aren't old enough to know their sexuality or gender identity and, if we speak over them, we aren't giving them the chance to show that they absolutely do know themselves and what they need. No one can advocate better for trans kids than trans kids. So, when asked on this topic, I do share what I know but I also hand over to organizations and protests like this, highlighting the work that they do. So, while I will always advocate for this cause, sometimes I believe the most effective way of doing this is by amplifying these young voices and listening to them.

How to be a good listener (yes, even to those who we think are wrong)

Being a good listener is an important skill and one that will aid you in all elements of your life. It will help you learn from and be connected to other human beings. And it will help you in those situations where you are wrong.

So, what makes a good listener? A good listener is someone who fully engages with the person they're speaking to, which means . . .

- they allow the other person the time and the energy to make their case without interrupting them.
- they are focused on what the person is saying, rather than being preoccupied with what they're going to say next.
- they value the other person's opinion and don't minimize their life experience.
- they go into a conversation knowing that they could be wrong, which leaves space for the other person to correct them and perhaps help to open up their mind.

In order to truly listen, we need to put ourselves on pause.

Putting yourself on pause might mean listening carefully to viewpoints that you disagree with. As I said at the beginning of this chapter, there's so much nuance to the big issues in life, and often there isn't a clear right or wrong side to things. There might even be a middle ground where you're both right.

You are always going to encounter people with different viewpoints from your own – that's a fact of life. But listening to them can still help your activism. If you're in a conversation with someone who has a different viewpoint from you – and you feel you have the energy to do so – listening to where they got those viewpoints from can be incredibly useful and important, even in those situations where you know – either because you have done the research or because it's about your lived experience – that you are right, and they are wrong.

Let's take the conversation surrounding transgender women's access to bathrooms and other traditionally gendered spaces. This is an example of how my body and existence has been politicized over the last decade. It's so upsetting and anger-inducing, and I know how wrong and damaging the beliefs upholding certain arguments are. But I do still try to listen, as it gives me clues as to what can be done to bring about change.

To explain how, I first have to give you a little bit of background on this long running and dangerous 'debate'. It's something that gets discussed all across the world, but as I live in the UK, I'll explain some of the views here that I have directly had to challenge or listen to. Under existing law, transgender people are allowed to use the toilet that best matches their gender identity[24] – so I can, legally, use a women's bathroom as I am a woman. But the government has been trying to challenge this right by putting forward various proposed laws. They are claiming that if people are allowed to self-identify as trans, then cisgender men will start using this as an opportunity to disguise themselves as women in order to access women's spaces. There is no data or real-world examples to support this theory *at all*, and 'debating' trans people's access to public spaces is regressive and incredibly dangerous.

For the trans community, seeing these conversations splashed over the front of newspapers and being discussed on television is to watch our freedom being taken away from us. We are afraid to go to certain places or wear certain things for fear of attack. When those at the very top are saying transphobic things, we can't even trust the police or any of the systems that are supposed to be in place to protect us.

The thing is, there *is* a very real threat to women's and girls' safety in society, but we know that these dangers come from the patriarchy and cis men, *not* trans people. Those in power could be spending their time looking for solutions to what's really going on, but that involves dismantling a power structure that has been in place for years and years. Instead, it's easier to use trans people to distract us from the real issues within our society that cause women and girls to be in danger.

I'm incredibly angry at what's going on, but when I feel in the right headspace to do so, I try not to be angry at the individuals who have fallen for this technique of using trans people as distractions. Instead, I try to focus on where they got their ideas from, and why.

I'll ask things like:

- Why do you think trans women are a threat to you?
- Where did this fear come from?
- What data or evidence do you have for this?
- Do you think your fear might be misdirected? Where does it really lie?
- What trans people do you know? How do you think these stories impact them?

I truly believe we should be creating safe spaces for conversations, where both parties are listening with the goal of understanding. When someone says something misguided or wrong, it's still important to have empathy for that person. Humiliating someone or making them feel silly for having a particular opinion is unlikely to bring them round to your way of thinking – in fact, it's likely only going to alienate them further, or put them in an angry place where they put their walls up and refuse to listen to your point of view. Having empathy involves understanding that the person who said something wrong is still a human being, with all their flaws and potential for mistakes, just like you.

We are all products of our environment who have been raised with different experiences and around different viewpoints. In the case of the transgender bathroom discussion, this person could have a history of trauma that's causing them to respond out of fear and believe the lies being peddled to them. If I can find out why they believe what they're being told and where that may come from, I can gently show them why they're wrong or guide them to resources where they can learn more. Instead of being angry at the individual for saying something harmful, often it's a lot more productive to think of the system surrounding them and how they came to this thought process. That way you can think about directing your energy towards changing that system instead.

This is tough, and listening requires energy – especially when you don't agree with what's being said. There are also people who are stubborn and say damaging things again and again and again. Trying to have empathy for them or get them to change their minds will expend a lot of your energy and damage your peace. It's why I spent so much of the last chapter really emphasizing the need to pick your battles and not waste too much energy trying to change the minds of people who will not budge on their viewpoints.

You *need* to keep checking in on yourself and your boundaries. While in some situations it's good to talk to people who disagree with you, you don't *have* to do this – particularly when someone's intention is to invalidate your personal experience and what you know to be true.

Take care of yourself first, always.

When you're wrong

In reality you will get things wrong, both in your life and on your activism journey. It's how you respond to this that truly matters.

If you've upset someone, it's your responsibility to find out why and resolve it. Whether or not you agree that what you did was harmful or wrong, if someone's hurt is a product of your action, that is on you. Our intention is not always our impact, and our impact matters.

Say someone tells you that you've said something sexist. Even if your intention was truly not to be sexist, the best thing you can do is *listen*. Find out the reasons *why* someone thinks what you've said was sexist. Don't just dismiss that person because your gut reaction is to disagree. The same applies for racism, or any other statement that could have offended or impacted a community or an individual in that community. The most effective thing you can do as an ally to that community is listen. This applies if you're from that community and if you're not.

The trick is to not just react immediately. Don't see being called out as an attack, as so often, it's truly not – it's a chance to learn. When given this opportunity to learn you could respond with, 'I'm sorry, I know it's not your job to do this for me, but if you could help me understand what I got wrong or how I offended you, then I can learn from it and move forward.'

And remember, you should always lead with 'sorry'. Regardless of whether or not it was your intention, if you've hurt someone, that was the impact. Every conversation is going to be different, so while it's hard to give you the precise words to say, one thing you should never do is frame it as, 'I'm sorry you feel that way.' That statement shows a complete lack of ownership of your actions. You could instead try, 'I'm sorry *my actions* have made you feel this way.'

We are all responsible for our impact on other people.

Ultimately, you need to view each time you're wrong as a learning opportunity. You've been given a chance to not do it again, and to ensure you don't blindly cause hurt in the future – that's a gift. The person who has been wronged will appreciate it if you show with all your heart that you've taken what they've said on board and are going to apply it in the future.

I have already told you how much my activism has helped me to understand myself and who I am. Hopefully you're beginning to see what I mean. Maybe you have begun questioning yourself and where your biases lie. Perhaps you've started approaching conversations with the understanding that you might be wrong, and you're ready to have your mind changed or opened up to another narrative. And maybe you've noticed in yourself a deeper empathy for the fact that every person and situation is complex.

One thing I have learned to accept about myself is that – just like everyone else in the world – I can't get it right *all* of the time. I don't expect that of everyone else, so why would I push that impossible ideal on to myself? We all have bias, and we are all a product of our own environments. The more you understand that you are a fallible human, capable of both success and failure, you can begin to become a better, more empathetic and more compassionate person. Rather than following gut reactions to things you see and hear, you'll understand that there are two sides – even three sides – to the truth.

Talking points

People are always going to get things wrong – we are all human. I hope this chapter has made you feel a little less afraid about making mistakes when entering into tough conversations. Navigating these discussions can be extremely complex and even when we have the best intentions and feel that we want to be someone who is empathetic, thoughtful and slow to react, we will all have days when that's simply not possible. All you can do is keep trying your very best, knowing that you deserve empathy and compassion in the same way as everyone else. And that includes being compassionate towards yourself!

Remember . . .

- **Consider who's in the room.** Are there people with lived experience being given a platform to speak? If not, is there a way you could help make them feel comfortable enough to speak?
- **Slow down.** If someone is speaking about a topic that makes you angry, take a step back and think empathetically about how best to approach them. Are you listening to where their views came from?
- **Be open to having your mind changed.** Sometimes there are two – or even three – sides to a story. Go into conversations with an open mind and be ready to understand other people's perspectives.
- **People get things wrong – including you!** It's important to offer empathy, as that's something we all deserve.
- **Know yourself.** Once you understand why you react the way you do in certain situations and give yourself empathy, the more empathy and understanding you can give to others.

5

We Need to Talk About...
Being the Killjoy

Killjoy: a person who deliberately spoils the enjoyment of others.

I used to think I was such a killjoy. When I first started talking about racism and highlighting both my experiences and the experiences of my community, it was 2017. I'd discuss these issues in interviews and on social media and it was a time when not a lot of people were talking about that stuff as loudly in the fashion and beauty spaces I was occupying. Today we see more models and actors discussing different causes they care about, but back then, it was a little different. I always felt like people didn't want to involve me in projects because I was talking about all these 'heavy things'.

I'd sometimes walk into a room and feel as if I represented the tough, bleak subjects I spoke about. It wasn't that I was doing anything wrong by bringing them up as they all *needed* to be spoken about, but at the time, it seemed like the industry wanted 'good vibes only', and I felt like I wasn't fun enough.

The industry has massively changed since then, as more and more of us within it are showing that you can be both. You can be someone who loves fashion and loves beauty, but who also wants to take a stand against the injustice in the world. That has made things a little easier. But ultimately I've learned to not let the idea of being a 'killjoy' get in my way.

I wouldn't say I've 'embraced' being a killjoy, as that would be letting my issues embody the wholeness of my being, but what I have learned is that when I'm talking about these topics and my experiences, there will always be people who don't want to hear it. This could be the same for you. There will always be people who try to use the word 'killjoy' to bring you down and stop you from speaking – don't let them. You have to recognize that they are only pushing that idea on to you as they don't like what you have to say.

Activists are seen as killjoys because they pop people's bubbles. They force people to look at a lot of really difficult stuff directly, and that isn't fun. Sometimes I wish I was more ignorant to a lot of the injustice in the world, as to not be aware of it all would make me so much happier. But then I wouldn't be living a life rooted in reality, which would mean I wouldn't be able to be a part of the fight for a better world.

Of course, it isn't 'good vibes' to know that all around the world there are people who are starving, children who don't have access to education and so much other suffering. This isn't happy stuff. But it is the reality of life. We have to have these uncomfortable conversations that no one wants to hear, as they are how change comes about.

It's not us who's the killjoy – it's the world.

Don't kill your own joy

It's easy to become consumed by all the injustice in the world when you have so much anger towards it. But you can't lose sight of yourself. I have definitely experienced this before, and it was during those times that I wasn't being a killjoy, but I was killing *my* joy.

I felt I didn't really exist outside of the struggle, and being silly or joyful no longer felt possible. My work and personal life centred around how painful and unjust the world was for trans people. And, today, those struggles remain. In 2023 – eight years after I first started speaking in public about my experiences – hate crimes against transgender people hit a record high in England and Wales.[25] There have been a number of recent high-profile attacks, including the murder of transgender teenager Brianna Ghey. In America, in 2022 more than 50 per cent of trans and non-binary youth in certain states considered suicide.[26] I could see the reality of these statistics playing out every day through the experiences of my friends and community. All I wanted to do was fight and scream about how unfair it all was. I couldn't lean into my joy as it felt like I'd be doing my community an injustice by doing so.

But it reached a point where I was numb, and where *everything* was dark and fraught. I had to spend some time focusing on myself and trying to bring back my natural silliness and joy. With time and work, I began to recognize that actually a big part of educating people and being an activist for my community is also about showing that trans people exist outside of trauma. Even though the injustices that make me want to fight and scream remain, we deserve to be seen in our wholeness, and showing that wholeness is a powerful political act. If tragedy is the only side of the trans experience that is visible, then how can we be seen as whole human beings?

The greatest thing I ever did for myself was move my activism away from frustration and allow people to see all of my different sides. I'm a silly person; I laugh a lot; I have a lot of joy but I was afraid to show it. Now? I try and show every part of myself. I host *Queerpiphany* on MTV. It's a fun, light-hearted show where we discuss the pop culture moments that affirmed our queerness with LGBTQIA+ celebrity guests. These moments have ranged from niche television storylines to iconic popstar performances, and it's all about showcasing how unique yet shared the 'coming out' process is for all queer people. The process of getting to a point where you're OK with or even happy with who you are is a wonderful thing. Doing the show has been an opportunity to enjoy this part of my identity and hopefully allow others to do the same.

This is all a part of my activism. I can host *Queerpiphany* one day, talk at the UN the next, then go and advocate for trans kids before turning up on the red carpet in a full latex look. I'm multifaceted, and I can be *all* of those things! Embracing my different sides has ultimately helped people connect with me and my cause.

You don't owe people *anything*. But embracing all parts of your humanity will not only help your activism but will also help you live your happiest life. If you show your *whole* self and someone still sees you as this two-dimensional killjoy, then that's on them.

Oppression surrounds us. I don't mean to sound bleak though – life is also an amazing thing to behold and full of wonderful things: music, theatre, movies, friends and laughter. Take a moment now to pause and think about all of the things that bring you joy. Maybe even make a note of them somewhere so that you can make sure you acknowledge them daily. If you find yourself getting lost in your cause, or you're in a period where all your conversations seem to centre around injustice, then it's time to take a step back and immerse yourself in something that brings you joy so you can find yourself again.

It's possible to gain a harmonious relationship of both righteous anger and joy. Change may often require rage, but it also cannot be sustained without love.

How to live in your wholeness:

- **Surround yourself with people who pull you up.** I'm a catastrophizer. I will go through the ten worst things that could possibly happen before even considering what could go right. My mind naturally goes to the negative before seeing the positive. But I have so many friends who help me prioritize the positive and refocus my mind.
- **Consider how you feel.** Remember in Chapter 1 when I said I'll take a moment to examine why I'm feeling certain things? I use that practice to recognize what brings me joy and, on the flip side, what makes me feel stressed, upset and overwhelmed. You can practise this in so many different ways. If you always feel exhausted and sad after you see a particular person, you could consider spending less time with them. Or, if you're going to the gym and doing a sport that makes you feel good, why not make time to do more of that? Embracing and recognizing what makes you happy will allow you to direct your time towards those things rather than the things that drain you.

- **Find the joy in your cause.** The poet, writer and civil rights activist Maya Angelou once said that she 'doesn't trust people who can't laugh'. And I really believe that in the most dire of situations one of the most defiant things you can do is find joy. It's your spirit refusing to be killed. You'll find laughter and joy are so prevalent on marches as, even though suffering is what tends to have brought everyone there, there's so much love to be found in uniting and being able to laugh in spite of it.
- **Live outside your cause.** Not everything you do has to be linked to your activism. Seek out books and TV shows that are silly or allow you to escape yourself. You don't have to be reading heavy non-fiction or watching documentaries all the time. Make sure your downtime is just that and seek out the things that make your body and brain properly switch off.

Pulling positivity from pain

I hate the thought of other people going through pain or trauma. I wish for a world where we are free from other human beings causing us harm. But as much as I hope you haven't experienced trauma – or that you won't – if you have it's so important to recognize that you are not alone. What has happened to you is both entirely unique to you and can also become a shared experience. By connecting with others and hearing each other's stories, we can take our pain and turn it into something powerful. With the support of others we can ensure that our trauma doesn't become all-consuming to the point where we don't have any control over it.

I've shared a lot of my own story of my past and my trauma. I've done so in the public eye as well as with those close to me. I wanted to be able to take the agony and anger out of my body and into the world. By doing that, I've learned some tough lessons along the way.

In my early twenties, at the very beginning of my transition, I met someone in a bar, and we went home together. After that evening we saw each other for a while, until he began to make me feel uneasy and I broke things off. He then persisted to stalk me for six months, which culminated in him breaking down my door and sexually assaulting me.

My whole life changed. For a very long time, I remained silent and didn't share how I was feeling. I felt like it was my fault and that what happened to me had made me dirty. I was so ashamed to speak up. I know now that it absolutely wasn't my fault, but those feelings didn't come from nowhere – they came from how I was treated in the aftermath of the attack. I called the police and was faced with the barrage of questions so many victims are subjected to – things like, 'What were you wearing?', 'What do you do for a living?' and 'How many sexual partners have you had?' None of these things mattered – I was attacked. But the people asking them were trying to scope out whether I might have brought this on myself. It was a disgusting way to treat someone, as no victim of rape or sexual assault has ever done *anything* to bring about their attack. All the blame lay with my attacker, yet the police and their questions made me feel like it was my fault.

Conversations surrounding rape and sexual assault have developed since then. Survivors have been sharing their stories and their subsequent mistreatment by the police – similar to my own – and fighting against it. But back then, the culture was very much one in which you were encouraged to keep quiet. By staying silent I got caught in a loop of shame – I didn't know others had gone through and felt the same things I had, and therefore I felt I was wrong for feeling that way. I tried for so long to bury how I felt.

This is such a natural reaction. Whether it's being bullied, facing sexual harassment on the street, or going through damaging and abusive relationships, we often think we have to 'keep calm and carry on'. We feel the need to hide our wounds. But when we do that, we become stuck – trapped within our own trauma.

I liken our subconscious to a cobwebby attic; in fact, I call it the attic of our soul. There are only so many things we can shove in there and ignore without ever properly processing them before they all start spilling out. It was only once I confronted the things I'd hidden in my own attic that I was able to heal. The process wasn't easy – just like cleaning an attic out, there are points where everything is splayed out in front of you and it feels dusty, suffocating and totally unmanageable. But once you do it, your whole house is better off.

One of the most important steps of this mental clear-out is showing what's inside to someone else. I know that sharing your trauma is incredibly difficult, and it can take time until you feel ready to do it. But once you find a way that feels right for you, it really does help. Before I spoke out, it was like I was trapped in a mental jail. I was finding it hard to connect to friends, to be relaxed on dates and to be vulnerable with partners, and keeping everything inside was only hurting me more.

I began to wonder, '*Why is this my burden? Should I really have to carry this around with me?*' In 2017, I wrote an article for the BBC about my experience of sexual assault. By that point I'd already been talking to some trusted friends, some of whom had been through similar experiences, and they really encouraged me to keep opening up. After the article came out I had so many women writing to me with their own stories. They offered words of encouragement, saying how brave it was of me to speak up. That spurred me on even further because it shouldn't be brave, and we shouldn't feel afraid to share our own stories, but we are because there are people who may not recognize your trauma and there may even be some who try to minimize it. I can't say that won't happen – it's a valid fear, and it's the reason why so many people don't speak up. But from my experience, it's worth trying. Even if you share your story knowing that not everyone will understand, remember that they don't have to for your feelings to be real.

By sharing, you *will* find people who understand. Great power can be found in speaking out. It helps others, but it also helps you. Speaking out made me feel like I was defying what happened to me and not allowing the experience to define me.

Speaking out can also be a way to root the anger and pain outside of your body and turn it into something constructive. It allowed me to highlight the mistreatment of women – and in particular trans women – by the police in these situations, as well as show that stalking wasn't just something experienced by celebrities. I'd found it difficult to recognize that I was being stalked, as I thought it was something that only happened to those in the public eye (which I wasn't at the time), so by sharing my story I could help others recognize the signs of stalking in their own cases.

Sharing our stories, particularly as marginalized people, is a way for us to show powerful people and organizations that they are not beyond criticism. The Black community and the queer community have been speaking out for a very long time about their mistreatment at the hands of the police. Then in 2021, a 33-year-old woman called Sarah Everard was kidnapped and murdered by a serving police officer in London. It triggered multiple other cisgender women to begin to speak out on their own experiences of being dismissed or mistreated by the police. This highlighted deep-rooted biases and unacceptable behaviours within the UK's police force, and investigations were then launched into how to address this. There's still so much more work to be done but, ultimately, the only way to show how the police aren't on our side was to share our experiences.

If you have experienced a trauma and you feel ready to share it, you could go to someone you feel safe with – that person we spoke about earlier who feels like home to you. This is a situation where I can't tell you how to best approach them as each and every experience is so unique, but what I can tell you is how much better you will feel for opening up to someone who cares.

You can also speak to service providers. I didn't know that there were charities that were out there that could help me, and if I'd known about organizations like Galop – a charity that works with LGBTQIA+ victims and survivors of abuse and violence – I would have felt much more supported. They offer much-needed emotional support, and they truly understand the gravity of these situations in a way that will help you rebuild your life. It's vital you get the support that's right for you, but remember that there is no pressure to share your trauma more widely if you don't feel comfortable doing so.

Being inspirationally contagious

Aged 19, I sat down and watched a documentary that changed my life. It was vibrant, unapologetic and fierce. While watching it, I felt like I was in a vortex where I was being encouraged and spurred on by history. For the first time, I felt like I was looking at myself.

That documentary was *Paris Is Burning*, which chronicles the ballroom subculture of New York in the 1980s. It follows African American and Hispanic gay men, drag queens and transgender women as they compete in competitions involving fashion runways and vogue dancing battles. The film shows their lives – we don't just see the colourful ballroom moments, but also get to hear from the scene's key figures, who talk about complex subjects including class, race and racism, gender identity and beauty standards. I drew such power from it.

Everyone in the documentary was incredible, but in particular I saw my dreams reflected in Octavia St. Laurent. She wanted to work in fashion and be a model, and she went on to do so. If I hadn't seen the documentary, or learned about Octavia and recognized how her dreams matched my own, I don't think I would have had the guts or the gall to have gone after what I wanted.

I got so much power from that documentary, and I know so many others in my community feel the same. Later, more role models entered into my stratosphere, from Janet Mock, whose book *Redefining Realness* was the first trans memoir I ever read, to Laverne Cox. Her character in the Netflix show *Orange Is the New Black* was one of the first times we saw a trans woman be presented with lots of layers and nuance on a high-profile show. Her presence really allowed me to feel a sense of pride in who I was. Her achieving that role made me feel I could achieve what I wanted for myself.

Then later, when I was in the public eye and often being trolled online or by the right-wing press, I would think of people like Nadia Almada and April Ashley, trans women who were put through hell by the British press.

Nadia was, at age 27, the reality TV show *Big Brother*'s first transgender winner, but was outed as a sex worker by the tabloid press after winning and retreated from the public eye after leaving the house. There was this sense that in Britain, we'd build up trans women and celebrate them, only to then destroy them later, upon realization of the reality of their existence.

I particularly remember drawing power from April Ashley's story. She was a model and actress, and one of the earliest people to undergo gender affirming surgery, in 1960. But her 'friends' outed her to the press, and she faced endless abuse as a result. Reading her story and learning more about her, I could see how heartbreaking the treatment she received was, but also how she held herself with such dignity and had this real sense of determination. She was inspirational to me.

And now, there's a whole new generation who say that they have been inspired by my work. They, in turn, will then inspire a new generation.

All of this has shown me that this hard work and the challenges of speaking out are worth it in *so many* different ways. The changes you make can set off a ripple effect, where you inspire others to go off and do their own work to make the world a better place. It's the opposite of being a killjoy – you are spreading the joy!

Even though you might not ever know the many ways that you have inspired people, you can be the spark.

I call this being 'inspirationally contagious'. It's that awakening in other people, where your words spur something in them. Being inspirationally courageous could look like . . .

- **telling people what you care about.** For example, if you volunteer on the weekend, you could tell people just how happy it makes you. It might inspire them to look into volunteering opportunities of their own.
- **discussing what you're learning about the world and yourself.** When other people see you so lit up and excited about your new-found knowledge, they might want to feel that way themselves too.
- **showing people who your role models are.** Let people know if you find a person or voice that speaks most to you and point people to their work. Or encourage them to find someone else whose words and voice light them up, and to share them with you!
- **being unapologetically yourself.** This is what it really all boils down to – being yourself in an unfiltered way. You can expand people's imagination by just being yourself, as there's only one of you and you're so unique. There's something disruptive about caring less about what other people think of you. It takes bravery, but the pay-off is great as it encourages others to follow in your footsteps and show all their sides too.

You can influence people – and spread joy – by simply being yourself.

Talking points

Repeat after me: I am my whole, wonderful self, and I deserve love and respect. I don't have to be consumed by my cause 24/7 to show that I care. Everything I've gone through has made me who I am today; I can draw power from even the bleakest of experiences. I am amazing.

Remember . . .

- **It's not us that's the killjoy, it's the world.** Sometimes we have to talk about hard things, and we shouldn't be made to feel ashamed of that or let it stop us from speaking up about the issues that matter.
- **Be your full self.** By bringing that self shamelessly into each and every conversation, you will feel freer and happier.
- **You are not your cause.** There are so many other elements that make you, you: so make sure the world sees them all.

● **Change takes time. But it also spreads.** By trying to craft the world you want to see, you will inspire others to not just accept what they've always known. Activism creates a butterfly effect that spreads far, in small and big ways.

Part 3

—

Let's Start the Conversation . . .

In the first part of this book, we spoke about you going out and finding your cause – the thing that fires you up and makes you want to change the world.

I know it can be overwhelming finding your cause when there is so much going on. So, I want to talk about some things that you might want to consider discussing and learning more about. These are all topics that have helped me to much better understand society, my activism and the sort of world I want to live in.

And now we can think about this together.

I'm going to outline some conversation subjects that I believe are really worth having. Not just with those around you, but also with yourself, as many of them are about questioning our environments and the way we've been raised. Everything that follows is a jumping-off point, as it doesn't just start and end here. When you just scratch the surface of a conversation, you miss out on so much nuance. The more we talk to each other and question where ideas around certain topics have come from and why we feel the way that we feel, we not only gain a greater understanding of a topic but can often feel more connected to those around us – even those who we think we disagree with.

So, let's talk . . .

6

We Need to Talk About . . . Systemic Injustice

If you open up social media or a newspaper today, it will more than likely be flooded with stories that are presented as either shocking one-off incidents, tragic attacks or acts of violence performed by one or a few individuals.

It would be fair to assume that the perpetrators were acting alone. But the reality is that nothing happens in a vacuum, and so much of what we see happening in this world is dictated by the systems that run it. We cannot underestimate the influence that governments, the media and powerful figures have on how we all behave. When those in power are upholding a system that's unfair, and favours one group of people at the cost of another, it's known as systemic injustice.

Some people – mostly those who benefit from these systems – are in denial about the existence and influence of systemic injustice, but the truth is that we all live in a world where, either consciously or subconsciously, our identities and actions are shaped by decisions made higher up the ladder.

By recognizing this reality, we can understand ourselves and the world more and have more empathy for others. It's important to know that people – even those who cause harm – are a product of their environment. Instead of punishing the people who are products of the system, we should be challenging the system itself.

Systemic injustice is everywhere, but the more we can recognize it, the more we can resist it.

Take whiteness and racism. Racism isn't something that just happens to individual people – it is a system, and it is in place to keep the most powerful at the very top. It's impossible to condense the roots of racism down into a paragraph when entire books have been written on the subject of Black history. But one of the key periods in history – one that has shaped the world we live in now – took place between 1532 and 1832, when at least 12 million Africans were taken from the continent to parts of America and the Caribbean as enslaved people, where they were forced to work for nothing growing tobacco and cotton. Huge amounts of money were made from their hard work, but paying them fairly would have reduced the profit being hoarded by those at the top. By treating enslaved people with violence and making them feel like they were worthless, those in power were trying to ensure that the enslaved wouldn't have the energy to fight and rally for better treatment. However, records show that despite their best efforts to keep the enslaved oppressed there was still tireless resistance and a number of successful slave rebellions.

Slavery was abolished a long time ago, but that doesn't mean that people don't still profit from those of us who are marginalized. The racism that we see play out today is part of the same system that continues to benefit the powerful. They want us exhausted so we don't challenge it.

There's a famous quote by the writer Toni Morrison that reads . . .

'The function, the very serious function of racism is distraction. It keeps you from your work. It keeps you explaining, over and over again, your reason for being.'

It's something I keep in mind when I meet people who don't want to engage in politics or the fight. I really can't blame those who are impacted by injustices for wanting to disengage from them. It's exhausting feeling like you have to spend your whole life fighting, rather than living – particularly when there are so many examples of how racial systemic injustice is happening across the world.

We can see it today within our prison systems. Prisons run by private companies are common in the UK, the US, Australia and New Zealand, and in these places there's a higher proportion of people from minority ethnic groups serving time.

The stats show that . . .

- in the UK, over a quarter of the prison population are from a minority ethnic group. This does not reflect the ethnic make-up of England and Wales. In 2023, the arrest rate for Black people was 2.2 times higher than for white people.[27]
- in the US, in 2022, Black people were admitted to prison at four times the rate of white people.[28]
- in Australia, the most marginalized group of people are Indigenous Australians, and Indigenous children are 17 times more likely to go to jail than non-Indigenous children.[29]

When a prison is run by a private company, the government is outsourcing a job to an outside company[30] and usually this saves them money in the long run. These private prisons charge the government per inmate, and therefore they benefit financially from both having more people in prison and keeping them in longer. And when a prison profits from people being in there, they have an incentive to keep them fully occupied.

Let's dig a little further now into our policing system and how it disproportionately targets Black people . . .

- In the UK, data released in 2022 showed that Black people are almost nine times more likely to be stopped and searched than white people.[31]

- In the US, Black adults are five times as likely as white adults to say they've been unfairly stopped by the police because of their race or ethnicity.[32]
- In New South Wales in Australia, excessive force such as wrist locks, arm restraints and ground wrestling was used by police on Indigenous Australians at a disproportionate rate over periods between 2018–20 and 2021–23. Indigenous people were involved in about 45 per cent of incidents where police used force, despite making up only about 3.4 per cent of the population.[33]

This treatment is all so clearly unfair . . . but yet it remains. The system has created a culture that makes people think this is OK. Media stories imply people of colour actually are more 'dangerous' and commit more crimes than white people, which in turn contributes towards public fear or suspicion of Black people. News reports then make people think this is 'fair' and justified treatment, and people of colour are framed in such a way that distracts us from what could *really* bring about change.

And all this benefits those with privilege, wealth and power, giving them even more privilege, wealth and power. So why would they try and stop it?

This is an example of systemic injustice that favours those at the top. It's huge and it's complex, but it's real.

I mentioned in Chapter 4 how trans people are often used as distractions, and this isn't something that just happens to my community. It's commonplace, and once you begin to recognize it, it can open your mind to injustice and how to talk about it. If you're aware of how powerful systems could be designed to distract from what's really at play, you can use that knowledge to talk about what *really* needs to change.

You'll find that when you begin to notice how systemic injustice plays out within society, you'll notice it everywhere. When there's a big news story dominating the headlines and your social media feed, try to analyse it with systemic injustice in mind. You can do this by . . .

- **reading as much as you can around a situation.** How is it being framed by different publications? How are people on the ground experiencing it? How does that differ from what the more mainstream publications are saying?
- **thinking about why and how this happened.** Everything has a backstory. Could there be a bigger cause behind this?
- **drawing a diagram in your head.** Where is everything pointing to? Who is benefitting from what's going on?

Brianna Ghey

I should say that, just because our systems can cause people to think or behave the way that they do, it doesn't excuse them for their actions. This isn't me shrugging and thinking, '*It's not their fault; they were made to do this.*' Ultimately we are all responsible for our own behaviours. When we consider the factors that led to a certain thought process or behaviour, it's not to find excuses but simply to be able to recognize a key part of the puzzle.

Take the tragic murder of Brianna Ghey. She was a 16-year-old transgender girl from Warrington, England, and she had dreams of being a beauty therapist. Two teenagers – including someone who had pretended to be her friend – have now been jailed for life for her murder after a pre-planned attack in February 2023. At the time, much of the conversation around her murder talked about it as a one-off despicable act, with all the blame lying solely with the teenagers.

Now of course her murder *was* down to the actions of the two teenagers. But how could the system that they were raised in have influenced them or contributed to their actions? This was a vital part of the conversation that was missing when the murder was reported by the media.

Kids don't just kill other kids without something having gone very wrong beforehand. There has to have been a series of things that led to this murder. In the run-up to killing Brianna, the two teenagers exchanged messages calling her transphobic names, and during the sentencing the judge said the murder was partly motivated by Brianna's transgender identity.[34] They targeted and plotted to kill Brianna because she was trans. When we live in an environment where trans people are regularly attacked and dehumanized by the media and the government, it creates a world where actions like this become normalized.

The way trans people are spoken about and treated in the press is violent. We are consistently misgendered, and 'debates' about whether we are 'real' men or women are commonplace. According to analysis by the transgender activist Shon Faye, in 2020 the British newspapers *The*

Times and the *Sunday Times* published over 300 stories about trans people – almost one a day – and they were all negative.[35]

When our human right to go to the bathroom that matches our gender is threatened, and when we are blamed for the huge problems of violence that women face, we are dehumanized. We are not painted as real people with real lives; as people who are loved and who love – instead we are seen as 'other' and as a threat.

That in turn encourages violence towards us. We see this happening to every marginalized community – the way those in power speak about illegal immigrants, for example, has an impact on the way that they are treated. Donald Trump – arguably one of the most influential people in the world – has called immigrants 'animals' and 'not human' in a 2024 speech,[36] while papers read by millions in the UK have referred to groups of refugees as 'swarms' and 'floods'.[37] These are real people who have often faced unimaginable hardship. They deserve respect and compassion, and they get this instead.

When someone in a position of power speaks in a cruel, dehumanizing way about a marginalized community, it sends the message to the general public that it's OK to disrespect them, mistreat them and – in the worst cases – kill them.

What can I do?

Very rarely is it just *one* thing that causes someone to believe or behave the way they do, but rather an overlapping tangle of different factors. But by recognizing and understanding the systems at the heart of society's behaviour, we can then think, 'Do I want to participate in that? Or do I want to use what I know to challenge this power?'

Imagine you're with someone who is shaking their head and angrily showing you a video of someone shoplifting. 'The papers are saying that it's an epidemic, that everyone is nicking stuff these days,' they say. The facts do back this up, and a greater number of people *are* shoplifting more than ever.[38] But could there be a system at the root of this problem? Is it right that the person is angry at the individuals shoplifting rather than talking about the cause? You could ask them . . .

- Why do you think someone might feel forced to shoplift for food, clothing and essential items?
- Are there any government policies that are leaving people in desperate situations?
- Why do we even have poverty when the number of billionaires is growing? Who is allowing this to happen?

Often we who oppose the system outnumber those that are imposing it.

Those in power will have to do more to support people in poverty if we recognize that it's not an individual's fault if they're driven by economic circumstances to steal to feed themselves or their family. Those in power will struggle to maintain public fear towards people of colour the more we all come together to challenge racism. Those in power will have to do more to protect women and girls from violence once we all come together and acknowledge that trans women are not the real threat.

Of course, the people in power don't want this. They don't want us to come together and fight the systems that they benefit from. There's so much strength in our community, and when marginalized people come together, we are resisting those in power and the system that has been in place for far too long.

And where do we start? By having conversations.

Talking points

Now that you've begun to recognize what systemic injustice is and how it plays out across the world, you can use that knowledge to examine who benefits from it and what needs to change. You could also look at how systemic injustice plays out closer to home in your school, college, workplace or community. Depending on what your cause is and the issues you want to lend your voice to, here are some questions you could begin to explore further:

- When you think about crimes such a shoplifting, what are some of the reasons people might commit them? Is there anything our government could do to prevent it from happening in the first place? For example, if there was more support for those in poverty, would they need to steal?

- What other ways does systemic racism play out across society? What messages are we told about those from minority communities? Who benefits from this?
- What messages are we taught about women, and the work that they do? Across the world, there's a gender pay gap where men are paid, on average, more than women for the same work. Why could this be?
- Do girls feel safe navigating the world? How about LGBTQIA+ people? What is it about the environment around them that might be making them feel unsafe?

7

We Need to Talk About . . . Reframing

Pride marches are vibrant and colourful. There's laughter in the air, music being blasted from speakers and rainbow flags swaying in the wind. There's also this overwhelming feeling of joyful defiance – a sense that we have all faced similar struggles and are coming together, despite it all, to find the light within us and let it shine. It's a day of freedom that comes from being encouraged to be ourselves in our entirety.

I will always remember watching a child play with their dad at one Pride march. This beautifully carefree, effeminate child, spinning and twirling in a princess outfit and being utterly themselves. It was a joy to see. Their dad wasn't forcing them to behave like a boy or fit into any box – he was just letting his child be *exactly* who they wanted to be.

When I was younger there were very few adults who allowed me to be free. I've always known that I'm queer – in fact, I first came out to a childminder when I was around the age of seven – but I was raised in an environment where I was encouraged to be the opposite of myself. So, I was swiftly told that I was confused and ushered into a closet of shame, where I was trapped until I was 14 years old. I had no community or role models, and because of Section 28 (see page 67) I rarely saw myself reflected in the media or in books. All around me queer people were being told to hide ourselves; told that we were so wrong that laws had to be put in place to protect others from us. If we did find any representation of ourselves, we were generally the butt of the joke and being mocked.

Like many other members of my community I learned to repress my queerness, and I diluted my way of being throughout my childhood and teenage years. So now when I watch a child being given the complete freedom to be themselves, it makes my heart sing.

That's how every child should feel – completely free to explore themselves and be exactly who they are.

I often hear people discussing trans rights say, 'Let kids be kids,' with this false idea that by discussing gender identity with them we are pushing them into making 'grown-up' decisions about who they want to be. But what I witnessed at Pride was exactly that – a kid just being a kid. A dad allowing his child to explore what makes them truly feel happy. There are so many people in this world who want us all to live by a rigid guidebook – one that tells us exactly who we should be and how we should behave. It's pushed on children now just like it was pushed on me then, but if we are forcing kids to live by a guidebook, that is the exact opposite of allowing them to just 'be a kid'.

We need to examine our own framework and what boxes we may have been pushed into. This is why I believe that activism is one of the ultimate tools of personal growth, as it allows us to dig deep inside of ourselves and question what has been placed there by others. If we all felt free to try things out and experiment with what we *feel* is right for us – rather than what we've been *told* is right for us – then we would have a much happier society. People bully others because they watch them living outside of the guidelines that they feel they have to abide by. This makes them angry and scared, so they lash out.

When you look at your own life, and your own upbringing, what boxes do you think you could have been pushed into? Have you been asked about marriage or whether you'll settle down some day without ever being asked whether you want those things? Were you pushed to play with dolls when you were younger when really you wanted to play with trucks? Is it expected that you'll go to university or follow the same career footsteps as your parents? In this chapter we're going to see how we can reframe what we've been told about our lives and instead think of the ways we could live differently.

We need to reframe . . . coming out

One of the hardest questions to answer when you are young is the dreaded, 'What do you want from your future?' That's a really big question with a lot of expectation hanging heavily over it – particularly at this time when there's so much uncertainty about the climate and what our financial futures will look like. It can feel muddled and confusing and like everything is coming at you *all at once* . . . but still, people want answers from you.

You will be asked what career path you want to follow; whether you want to get married; or whether you want to have children. Often questions like these make the assumption that you are going to do what's considered 'normal' (though of course there's no such thing) and that you'll be straight and end up with someone of the opposite gender.

And maybe you will. Or maybe you won't. Or maybe you'll go through a period of your life where you feel you're one sexuality, and then you'll meet someone similar to you and be more attracted to them and lean into another sexuality. No matter what the future holds, and even amidst a barrage of questions it's important to remember . . .

You don't have to have all the answers. Not yet. Not ever.

Remember when I said that activism and all of these important conversations you're having are tools for personal growth? This is what I mean. Once you begin to recognize the pressure that is placed on us from oppressive systems you can free yourself from it. You can carve out your own new way of being – one that allows you to change your mind and have freedom to follow your own passions and desires.

One of the positive things about the world we're currently living in is that there's so much more awareness of different identities, different sexualities and different ways of being. But what also comes with this is a pressure to identify with one in a concrete way, and for some people this might come easily – but not for everyone, particularly as so much of who we are is fluid and changes over time. You may know exactly who you're attracted to or what gender you are, but you don't have to, and neither does anyone else. We need to leave space for fluidity.

Regardless of how we personally identify, we can all tear up the rule book. The idea that there are just two genders – male and female – is a prison for a lot of us. The idea that there are boxes for how we should identify is so limiting and finite, and it's really freeing to let go of that. I remember the first time that I saw drag queens in a Soho club when I was a teenager. I felt like life had gone from black and white to full, vibrant colour! I loved how defiant they were, sticking a middle finger up to society and to the idea that they had to dress or behave how they'd been told to behave just because of the gender they were born as. It was a similar feeling when I first met other trans people – the freedom of self that they embodied was so beautiful to me. Society has largely been built around this idea of binary gender and having to stick with the identity we were born with.

Being trans is bringing who you truly are to the surface. What could be more beautiful?

But you don't have to be transgender or go on that journey to feel empowered to break free from gender-conforming boxes. You could be a cis straight man embracing more feminine ways of dressing; or a lesbian woman who wants to dress in a more masculine way; or a non-binary person who wants to switch it up and dress in a way simply based on however you feel that day. We should be who we want to be. It's so glorious that because of those who came before us and challenged what we've previously been told we now have so much more freedom to express ourselves.

OK, but what *are* you?

While we have come a long way, there is still some way to go. And unfortunately you will always find people who want you to define who you are in a way they understand. They want your life to be wrapped up in a bow and made easily digestible. But that's not the reality. It's like when someone asks, 'What do you do for fun?' – it can't always be answered in a simplistic sound bite that people tend to expect of you.

Take coming out – why is that something we're still asking people to do? Why should that information belong to other people? We see celebrities being challenged on their queerness all the time – journalists ask them awkward questions in interviews about who they sleep with and fans demand it of them on social media, with lots of celebrities feeling great pressure to comment on their sexuality.

Kit Connor, an actor in the Netflix series *Heartstopper*, was made to tweet about his bisexuality in 2022.[39] Fans were demanding to know whether he was gay after appearing in the show, which highlights the lives of LGBTQIA+ people. Why should that have to be public knowledge?

Even when we do come out, we're often questioned over and over again. We will start new jobs or move to new places, and people will ask us about our sexuality. But why? When I came out as gay, I wanted to do so to disarm people. I was being bullied in school and I thought if I could just have it out there in the open, then it was information that couldn't be held against me. If I could fake it enough and show them that I was proud of being queer, then they would leave me alone. But that meant I came out before I was ready. I wasn't actually proud yet. I hadn't had the time and space to work on myself. I was coming out on someone else's terms because of the bullies, rather than because it was what I wanted.

Unfortunately my experience is common, even today. Often people are – for many different reasons – pressured to disclose something that they haven't even come to terms with themselves. The reality is that no one should have to come out before they're ready, or if they don't feel safe to. But so many people do give in to the pressure. We need to ask ourselves why. Why is there an expectation on queer or trans people to tell others if they're not straight or cisgender? It's not like we're harming anyone by not coming out!

If someone does want to come out and wants to talk about it, then that's great. Let's talk about gender and sex! What we don't want is to keep fostering this idea that this very personal information is something that needs to be public.

People forget that these identities are man-made. These

are boxes *we've* created. These words – straight, gay, pan, bi – these are words that we have made up to encapsulate infinite feelings, when throughout our lives we may change. So why is there so much pressure to know and to come out? Why do we demand that of ourselves and each other?

How to have the freedom to explore your gender or sexuality

- **Enjoy the journey.** The opposite of the word 'pride' is 'shame'. And the antidote to shame is to enjoy your sexuality and your gender identity. These are joyful things; draw happiness and love from them. They're there for you, as an individual, to discover, and you don't need to do this for anyone else.
- **Remember, no one knows you better than you.** We can share and discuss our similarities, but just because one person experiences their gender and sexuality in a certain way doesn't mean you have to do the same. There's no one way of being.
- **See your gender identity and sexuality as feelings, not actions.** Don't feel you have to do certain things or act a certain way in order to justify yourself to other people. Take your time to explore these feelings and identify what works for you.

Gravitate towards the situations and people that feel like freedom.

Transitioning

When it comes to disclosing your identity as a trans person, one of the most difficult things about that conversation is the questions that come with it. Often the person is inundated with questions that they may not have the answer to yet, with one of the most common ones being, 'Do you want *the* surgery?'

This can be as much of a big question for the person coming out as it is for those around them. There needs to be an understanding that the person is transitioning because they want the answers, not because they have them.

It was difficult during my transition because I didn't have so many of the answers. I was being asked all these questions and I felt like I had somehow been deceiving people. They wanted to know everything. It was as if I was keeping secrets to myself, and that was really not the case. I was still questioning and exploring who I was, and I needed the space to do so. Transness, just like sexuality, is a feeling. Just because one trans person transitions one way doesn't mean you have to copy that exact model. There is no rulebook.

If a friend or someone you know is questioning their sexuality or gender, here are some tips that I hope will help you navigate these conversations:

- **Don't ask constant questions.** This often isn't helpful, as they may not know the answers themselves. They don't have to know everything about how their transition or sexuality will look – not yet. But equally, don't try to find answers or solutions for them yourself. It's OK to say, 'I don't have all the right tools or information, but I am willing to go on this journey with you and be the support that you need.'

- **Be beside them on their journey.** When I came out as trans, I didn't know what my life as a trans person was going to look like, and neither did my friends, so it was an opportunity for us to come together. Don't leave anyone to explore their new experiences by themselves. This is a moment to connect, not fracture. You could suggest going along with them to things like Pride – or other events for them to meet their community – as a support and ally.

- **Look at the world through their lens.** If someone comes out to you or gives you information about their identity, try to put yourself in their shoes. Be aware of the political landscape and how that might impact them. When you are coming out or transitioning, you may be changing your appearance or stepping into a new way of being that is more authentically yourself. This brings comfort but also self-consciousness, and a great friend will pre-empt what you might need. For example, getting on public transport can be intimidating, so you could offer to travel to an event together.

- **Check in on them.** I had friends who, during the early days of my transition, would explain to me what the crowd would be like wherever we were going. They would say, 'There might be a lot of straight masculinity there – how do you feel about that?' as they knew that could be daunting for me. They'd ask, 'Do you feel resilient enough?' and keep that up even during the event, offering me moments to step away from the crowd and have breaks.
- **Don't say, 'It's just a phase.'** It's likely not just a phase. And even though some things might be phases it doesn't mean they're a negative thing. Even as an adult, I go through phases, but it doesn't mean that those phases aren't a part of me. I prefer to call them 'eras', as they are not permanent but are still a part of us.

There's a lot more guidance now, and the information is much more readily available for people taking these journeys than it was when I was younger. For example, in the UK there's Mermaids, the charity I work with closely, which support trans, non-binary and gender-diverse youth and have a phone line where you can talk totally confidentially to their support team. There's also the Proud Trust, which organizes local LGBTQIA+ groups to bring people together. (For more support look to the back of the book, where I've listed more organizations doing amazing work.)

I've shared my personal experience with you, but I also know that when friends come to me for advice, I need to adapt it to suit them – there isn't a one-size-fits-all approach or situation. But one thing I would love for everyone is if we could distinguish between coming out and confiding, as so often when someone is first questioning their gender identity, it's not that they're coming out and saying they know precisely who they are – they're telling you they're exploring that and going on a journey. At that point, they need the tools and support to go on that journey, rather than the pressure to know right in that very second everything about themselves and who they are.

We should allow ourselves and those around us to blossom in each and every era of our lives.

What to talk about . . .

You might, after reading this chapter so far, have some idea of what coming out feels like for the people in your life. Or you could be gaining a deeper understanding of how you're feeling within yourself. If this is something you want to start learning and talking about more, here are some questions you could explore further:

- Why do we expect people to come out if they aren't straight? And why do we expect them to have all the answers about their gender or sexuality? In what way does history play into this?
- Is there systemic injustice at play here? If people felt more free to be fluid with their sexuality, why might this make those in power fearful?
- How are people treated when they come out? Do we allow people the space to explore themselves, or do we try and put them into boxes?
- What messages are we told about bisexual people? How much do we understand about those who consider themselves asexual? What do we hear about transgender or non-binary people in the media? Are these messages coming from those with lived experience themselves?

We need to reframe . . . stereotypes

One of the most amazing things about human beings is that we are multidimensional objects. I am continually surprised by the people that I meet after I get chatting to them and learn their interests and their passions. It's easy to make assumptions about people based on how they look and how they choose to dress – whether they're covered head-to-toe in tattoos, wearing a pretty floral dress or a football shirt.

Where do these assumptions come from? We all make guesses based on someone's appearance. This is a natural process, but it's important to recognize that they're often based on stereotypes. Stereotypes are held about almost every group in society. These are widely held, fixed ideas that assume people will behave in a certain way because of things such as their appearance, gender, sexuality or race. These beliefs impact us in different but equally damaging ways.

We need to be having conversations that break stereotypes down. When we begin doing this, we will see each other as whole humans capable of being many different things. We are complicated beings, and there are so many different ways of existing that aren't dependent on things like race and gender. By examining stereotypes and discussing them, we can begin to recognize how they can hold us back or stop us from getting to know the wholeness of someone.

Why women should be trillionaires

We so often approach gender identity as if it has to fit into a cookie-cutter mould. Although we are starting to see some improvements in recent years, if you look in most children's clothing and toy shops, the idea that certain colours, hobbies and interests are for girls (pink, dolls, toy kitchens and so on), and others are for boys (blue, dinosaurs, cars and even toy guns) is still everywhere. From such an early age, gender roles and stereotypes that define girls as nurturing and boys as violent are pushed on us. There's little room left for waiting and seeing who that child grows into and what they naturally gravitate towards. It's telling women they should be a wife, or that they should be a mother, and men that they should be 'macho' and 'manly' with no space for emotion or vulnerability.

Remember how I said that a lot of the systems and stereotypes are there for a reason – to keep those in power at the top? Ensuring that we uphold gender roles is all part of this. Our economy is built on women taking on unpaid caring roles.

Caring for children or elderly relatives is continuous hard work that is often taken on by a female family member. It isn't recorded or measured, because it's seen as something that should be done for free as a mark of love or care within a family. But one estimation found that if women in the US alone earned minimum wage for their unpaid work, they would have earned $1.5 trillion, collectively, in 2019.[40] That estimate was before the pandemic hit, when schools and other public facilities were closed, sending children home for their lessons. Who do you think shouldered most of the responsibility for home-schooling?

If this work wasn't done, what would happen? And if it was recognized as valuable work that deserves to be paid for (which it is), who would this impact?

With 88 per cent of the world's billionaires being men,[41] how do you think they benefit from this unpaid labour?

Studies in the US and Canada have shown that married men are healthier, wealthier and happier than single men[42] but that the opposite is true for women, where single women are shown to be happier than married women. How could the traditional roles and expectations placed on women when it comes to caring for others play into this?

When we talk about misogyny, what we mean is a hatred or prejudice against women. We see it at an individual level and as part of a wider systemic issue. Misogynistic views shame women who break free from traditional roles – and they do so as a means to keep everything exactly as it is. Why? Because the current structures in place are hugely beneficial to a small group of people.

This is the same way of thinking as we discussed earlier when discussing systemic injustice. Racism can't be separated from misogyny; it can't be separated from transphobia; and it can't be separated from ableism. All forms of oppression are wrong, and they benefit this same small, powerful group.

You'll begin to notice similar strands in all these conversations, particularly in the ways that those in power push back by trying to shame, exhaust and divide us. Throughout this book – and in all the conversations you're having – I want you to be constantly questioning, '*Who is it that benefits from this?*'

Toxic male influencers

Recently there's been a rise in male influencers who flaunt their wealth, showing off their fast cars, private jets and yachts. They talk about how other men can get a lifestyle like theirs, and push the idea that to be masculine you should be wealthy, influential and sexually dominant.

They believe that men hold more value than women, and spout dated and damaging views about women. They tell their audience that women 'belong in the kitchen' and that women should be subservient to them and do everything they say. These views are hugely misogynistic but are, unfortunately, being believed by their impressionable audiences. As, often, fans of these influencers are boys who have turned to online content as they feel lost or unhappy. This sort of content tells them that they are unhappy because of 'woke' culture and feminism, which are stripping them of their rights. It's all untrue but does appeal to those who feel isolated, bullied or alone. Teachers have reported that boys in their classrooms are parroting similar views to these influencers, as well as speaking to female staff and fellow pupils in a bullying and domineering way.[43] New data has revealed that Gen Z men and boys in the UK are more likely than older generations to believe that feminism has done more harm than good.[44]

These views don't just harm women, though – they harm everyone. They tell men that they have to mould themselves into this hyper-masculine version of themselves, that they can't express emotion and that their value to this world only lies in making as much money as possible.

So how can we respond to people who support and repeat these views? How can we approach these situations with a little more empathy and understanding, and help them see that what they're saying is wrong? How can we change their minds?

Say you notice that a friend of yours is reposting this sort of content, or they're starting to speak or act like these influencers. What can you do?

- **Assess the situation.** As we discussed in Chapter 3, when it comes to having these tricky conversations, you have to protect your own energy first. It's not your job to change someone's mind – particularly if it's going to come at the cost of your own mental health. Can you face having this conversation?
- **Try to understand.** Lead with questions rather than from a place of attack. Don't say to someone, 'You must be a misogynist because you follow this person.' Instead, ask them, 'What do you see in this man?' and 'How do this man's values reflect your own?'

- **Lead them to their own conclusion.** Don't spell out the issues with what they're saying. Instead, guide them there. You could say, 'This video says this about women – do you really think that's correct when it comes to the women you know in your life?'
- **Walk away if you need to.** Even if you initiated the conversation, you don't have to remain in it, particularly if someone is getting angry or you don't think they're listening to you. You could say, 'I've made some of my points, let's revisit this another time,' and check out of the conversation.

We have made such strides in breaking down traditional gender roles. We will keep moving forward, one step at a time. But there will always be those who want to keep things as they are, and who will make attempts to squash our progress. While it's disheartening that they have such influence, there are also so many people shouting loudly about how deeply wrong they are! This in turn is changing the minds of those who may have fallen under their influence. The more we speak out against people like this and challenge their views, the more we are showing the power of conversation.

Our collective voice is louder than theirs.

Code-switching

Stereotypes infiltrate every part of our lives, not just gender roles. I'm of mixed-race heritage, and when I was younger, I would often find myself moving between mostly white spaces and largely Black spaces. But I didn't really feel like I fitted in with either. When I saw the Black side of my family, they had conversations about parts of Black culture that I didn't understand, as I hadn't grown up around it. But I also didn't feel like I belonged with my white family members or in white spaces either, as I looked and felt different. Trying to fit in with either side felt pointless.

When I talk about 'white spaces', I don't just mean places where the majority of people are white. In many European countries, as well as Australia and the US, all spaces are white spaces – not just physically but also in terms of representation and power. When the most represented group is white people, and when we are shown and taught about the world from the white perspective, this is how power is gained.

Think about it . . .

- The current curriculum in schools teaches history through a whitewashed lens that makes white people and their history more prominent than anyone else. This means people of colour so often don't see themselves and their stories represented in history.
- In our workplaces white men are over-represented, and despite efforts to make boardrooms more diverse the

number of white men in in the 'top 40' roles at FTSE 100 companies is actually increasing.[45]

- Throughout history, women in the art world had to produce their art under the guise of being a white male in order for it to be seen and considered 'great'. This still carries on today, with the worst-represented group in the US art world being women of colour.[46]

- In publishing in 2023, 72.5 per cent of people working in this industry in America were white. How could this impact what books are published? And if the books being published feature mostly white faces, and white characters, how could that affect someone growing up?[47]

White spaces are spaces that don't challenge the status quo, and that don't prioritize or celebrate diversity.

Considering this – is it any wonder that as I got older, I noticed that my Black friends and I would change ourselves when we were in white spaces? We would alter how we spoke, dressed or behaved in an exhausting attempt to fit in with the unwritten rules that exist within society – rules that uphold certain stereotypes about different races, and rules that have been dictated by white experience. I learned that there's a word for this: code-switching. It's prevalent in most minority groups, and originally the term was coined to refer to switching between different languages and ways of speaking.

Now – particularly as part of the Black experience – the term has moved beyond language and applies to all sorts of things that someone might do to try to fit in.

Code-switching could look like . . .

- changing your natural hair style or dressing differently to fit in with other people in your school, college or workplace.
- toning down your mannerisms or expressions.
- changing the way you speak.
- asking people to call you by a nickname, or a different name, as others might find your name hard to pronounce.

It's a pressure that comes from prioritizing how society wants us to be rather than who we actually are, and it's ultimately to your own detriment. It means we're not able to show **our whole selves,** and it gives others permission to expect us to be less of our own selves to be seen as professional or be a part of a group. By code-switching we are upholding the message that the way we are isn't acceptable or professional or appropriate and that we need to change to fit in.

The tough thing is people code-switch – both consciously and unconsciously – as a survival tactic. It's not as simple as saying, 'Just stop code-switching,', particularly when you consider . . .

- **Name-based discrimination.** In a 2021 US study, economists sent 83,000 fake job applications to a slew of major companies and found that white-sounding names get selected for job interviews more than Black ones.[48] This has led to 20 per cent of candidates trying to work their way around discriminatory hiring practices by changing their names on applications so as to sound 'less ethnic', as well as to sound younger or like another gender.[49]
- **Hair-based discrimination.** We spoke earlier about how school uniform policies had been used to discriminate against pupils with Afro hair, and this continues in work and education spaces today. Stories have been shared from individuals being told to take their braids out 'because employers wouldn't like it' to grooming policies stating that 'unusual hairstyles, including spiky hair, Afro style' wouldn't be accepted.[50]
- **Fear of abuse.** A Stonewall report found that in the UK, 35 per cent of LGBTQIA+ staff have hidden or disguised their sexuality or gender identity because they were afraid of discrimination.[51]

Everyone should feel able to bring their whole self into all facets of their lives. We need to break away from the idea that certain ways of being and living are preferable. We should all be allowed to act however we feel is most

comfortable and authentic to us regardless of whatever
environment we find ourselves within.

- **Look into unions and organizations within your work
  or school.** Is there an LGBTQIA+ society you could
  join? Or a BAME workers union? What policies are
  already in place and how could you all come together to
  change them?
- **Join a wider union.** If you look beyond your specific
  workplace, are there any unions you could join
  that could support you? For example, GMB Union
  UK campaigns and fights for better rights, pay and
  conditions for Black, Asian and minority ethnic workers
  by campaigning and lobbying the government on
  workplace issues, as well as working with individuals to
  improve standards in specific work forces.
- **Be aware.** If you want to be a strong ally and are
  someone who doesn't have to code-switch, then it's
  vital that you monitor the spaces you're in. If it's your
  workplace or school, watch out for discriminatory and
  offensive comments. You could shut these down yourself
  or speak to someone higher up when you witness
  them. Always consider how certain environments and
  messaging could make others feel.
- **Talk about it.** The more everyone is aware of code-
  switching and where it comes from, the more
  everyone – not just those directly impacted by it – will
  be able to recognize how unfair it is and work with you
  to bring about change. That being said, as allies we

should also be sure to never accuse someone of code-switching or assume that someone is. It's important that none of us feel that our expression of self is being policed.

We need to reframe . . . beauty standards

When do you feel at your most beautiful? I want you to really think about this question. Is it when you're wearing your favourite outfit and someone takes a great picture of you? Or when you've had a fresh haircut? Or is it when you're laughing so hard and have the biggest smile plastered across your face?

A friend asked me this question recently. Considering I work in the fashion industry, she might have expected me to say that I felt my most beautiful during a photoshoot or at an event I've walked the red carpet for. But for those events I've got a make-up artist, a hairdresser, a stylist and more all working as a team to make me look the way that I do. Then once I've spent hours getting ready, there's the professional photographers who know all about good lighting, and finally there's often re-touchers editing the image afterwards. What emerges from all of that work is essentially a product – and I don't feel at my most beautiful when I am a product.

I feel at my most beautiful when I have no make-up on, my hair is pulled off of my face in braids and I am laughing with my friends. They look at me and they see me, and I feel safe, accepted and enough.

We're so often shown one type of beauty in magazines, films and TV shows, and on social media. As women we are told that to be beautiful is to be thin and white, with a small, button-like nose – think of Disney princesses like Cinderella, or the classic Barbie doll. These are known as Eurocentric beauty standards, where these features are considered the benchmark of what is beautiful.

But these beauty standards exclude the (just as beautiful) features of women of colour. Many Black women feel the pressure to chemically straighten their hair so it appears more like that of white women. And, despite many of these products being illegal in the UK, creams that bleach and lighten the skin are still popular and for sale in some places.[52] It's also worth noting that many of the filters on social media that are there to make us look 'better' do so by slimming down our noses, brightening our skin and making our eyes look bigger.

We absorb all of this, internalize it and then hate ourselves for not matching that false ideal. That hatred then has a huge impact on how our lives play out and what we think we deserve.

During my childhood, I had internalized racism. I'd faced so much cruel bullying about my facial features and my skin that I didn't have any way to understand that they were beautiful. During my teenage years, diets were promoted everywhere I looked – from the pages of magazines to the adverts on television. There was this pervasive message that the only acceptable body type was thin. In my twenties – and in the early days of my transition – I faced so much transphobia. These overlapping experiences had a huge impact on how I viewed myself, and when I looked in the mirror, I couldn't see anything beautiful – instead, all I could think about was what I needed to change to match the standards that had been laid out for me.

My obsession over how I looked and picking apart every tiny thing about myself is known as body dysmorphia. This was also coupled with gender dysphoria, which for me was a debilitating sense of dread about my appearance, particularly when I examined the parts of me that pertained to the gender I was assigned at birth. All of these feelings led me to convince myself that I wasn't worthy of love or happiness. I subconsciously told myself only 'beautiful' people deserved those things, and as a result of this I ended up in abusive relationships. At the time, I felt it was what I deserved. Considering the things I had been told about myself, I started to believe that I was 'lucky' to be in a relationship at all – even one that was toxic and damaging.

I'm now much more at peace with how I look. But I have had multiple cosmetic procedures – alongside gender affirmative surgeries – in order to feel this way. I've asked myself, '*Why did I feel I had to do all of that, in order to be complete?*' It was partly survival, but there was also undoubtedly an aesthetic element to it. I feel so much calmer now about how I look. But I'm also very aware I shouldn't have had to go to the degree that I did in order to feel safe and happy.

Setting your own standards

Conversations surrounding beauty standards are complex and nuanced as while these standards cause so much damage and need to be dismantled, we also have to be careful not to criticize one another.

This goes back to how two things can be true all at once. We can know that, as women, the pressure to remove our leg, armpit, pubic and even facial hair isn't fair, while at the very same time feeling happier in our appearance when we do so. Or we might enjoy and find it empowering and fun to wear make-up, while also recognizing that by doing so we are conforming to toxic beauty standards.

We still live in a world where beauty standards reign. We have to be mindful of that fact and be gentle with ourselves and others. Just because one person does something with their face, body or hair doesn't mean they should expect you to do the same. And equally, if we feel confident breaking away from beauty ideals, we shouldn't be looking down on others who haven't reached that stage of acceptance within themselves yet.

Take the Kardashian-Jenners. They're a family made up of some of the most famous women in the world, with have a combined following of 1.2 billion on Instagram.[53] They have been criticized for upholding impossible beauty standards, as they have bodies that are incredibly hard to replicate without plastic surgery and faces that resemble filters popularized on social media platforms. Because what we see of them on social media is often so image based, they are accused of being bad role models. People criticize them for encouraging their fans to do dangerous things to themselves in order to look like them.

They make a lot of people incredibly angry. But perhaps instead of directing your anger towards them and other women who may look like them, it would be better to think about why we expect women in the public eye to be role models in the first place. Why do we expect them to represent every single woman in the world?

Surely all women should be able to present themselves however they want? The Kardashian-Jenners are also not immune to impossible beauty standards, and they too struggle with what we're told it takes to be acceptable and attractive within our society – Kourtney has had to deal with trolling for posting bikini pictures after having a baby,[54] and Khloé has been open about having had an unhealthy relationship with food from a young age, and being aware of online perceptions about her looks.[55] Kim has said 'I don't love my butt and my hips being so big' and that she 'totally [has] insecurities.'[56]

Even those who embody the 'perfection' we are told to strive for will struggle to fit the mould.

It's perfectly OK if you feel better with make-up than without, but it is worth considering *why* you feel that way. It's the same with shaving – if you feel more comfortable with shaved legs, that's no problem, but think about *where* that came from. We may feel the need to play into society's expectations in order to be seen and appreciated, and that's an incredibly difficult thing to admit, never mind push back against.

When having these discussions, the aim is not to feel ashamed of ourselves for buying mascara or wanting to experiment with different beauty trends. Instead, it's to get to the bottom of why we want to do this. Once we recognize this, the freer we will feel to make the decision as to whether or not we want to participate in that system.

And it's not just society's expectations we need to think about. Throughout history, numerous big brands and corporations have been able to influence beauty standards and the beauty choices we make by marketing their products in a particular way to make us think we need them, and to make us believe we are investing in an aspirational lifestyle or a 'better' version of ourselves. Typically, their goal is just to sell more product.

> When we're told something about ourselves needs 'fixing', who is it that is telling us that? What are we being sold by disliking it? Who benefits from that?

The need for representation

I remember my very first campaign. It was with fashion brand Uniqlo, and my face was on billboards and posters all over central London. It was the first time I'd seen a Black trans person in a huge fashion campaign. It was such a pivotal moment, and it made me feel like I could do absolutely anything.

Then when I booked a job with L'Oréal, I was the first trans woman to ever work with them on a campaign. That was powerful and a really positive step forward. It was a testament to the fact that beauty isn't just about the way you look, but instead the stories we have to tell. I hadn't, at that point, got access to a lot of the procedures or medical aspects of my transition that I wanted to, and I was speaking about and representing being a Black trans woman. Before that there weren't many brands using a diverse cast of models within their campaigns and adverts. I came into the public consciousness at a time when there was a woeful lack of representation, and it was something we really needed.

Today, representation is so much greater. Being able to see marginalized communities represented in adverts and on television can rewrite damaging stereotypes and challenge the idea of Eurocentric beauty standards in such a positive way.

It brings up questions about where the idea of beauty comes from and how it is woven into the fabric of society. Simply being present and visible means that other people can see themselves reflected, and they will hopefully end up feeling less pressure to measure themselves up to something that's completely unattainable.

What can you do to feel more beautiful within yourself?

- **Diversify your feed.** One of the great things about social media is that it's broken down some barriers and allowed us to celebrate and appreciate new forms of beauty. Before, the faces we were shown were the ones who fit the beauty standard and were selected to be in movies, TV and magazines. Now we have access to so many more people who not only represent other forms of beauty, but who are celebrated for more than just how they look.

- **Watch out for the comparison trap.** If you find that you're always on social media and comparing yourself to others, look into cutting back how often you're on there. Also consider who you're comparing yourself to – could they also feel insecure about they look? Is how they look even real, or are they using filters or altering themselves in some way? Take a step back and examine whether you're unfairly comparing yourself to something impossible.
- **Make a list of all the things you find beautiful about yourself.** Make sure a big part of the list focuses on the things that aren't external. Are you a good friend? Have you taught yourself a new language? Beauty comes in so many forms, not just how we look.
- **Be aware of beauty trends.** If you're tempted to follow a beauty trend, you should take a step back and question why you want to follow it. If you did manage to change yourself in some way for the trend, what's next? There will always be another beauty trend, and when one ends, another one begins. What would our lives look like if we kept chasing them? What would we miss out on?
- **Appreciate each other's uniqueness.** Do we want a world where we all look the same? Or can we start to appreciate that beauty comes in a huge variety of forms? When we can celebrate the unique beauty in others, it's easier to recognize it in ourselves.
- **Look to older role models.** For so long we've been told that beauty is tied up in youth, but ageing is a beautiful

process that brings so much wisdom. There are now so many powerful role models challenging the idea that youth equals beauty, from model and actress Pamela Anderson not wearing make-up at Paris Fashion Week, to Jennifer Coolidge's acting career going from strength to strength as she ages.

Talking points . . .

Now that you've begun to recognize the prevalence and problem of beauty standards, you could use that knowledge to help others feel more beautiful too. If this is a cause you want to lend your voice to, here are some questions you could be exploring further:

- When it comes to the celebrities we aspire to look like, what do they tend to have in common? In what ways is this level of beauty reached? Is it possible for everyone or only a select few? Is it pushing a beauty standard that suggests that one way of looking is preferable to another?
- Do we want to live in a world where everyone looks the same, or would we prefer to live in a world where our differences are celebrated?
- If we stopped feeling bad about ourselves and all suddenly magically felt amazing about ourselves, what industries would suffer?
- When people feel upset by their appearance, what could be causing that? Could it be the comparison trap?

When it comes to
beauty, we have
to stop looking at
ourselves as crabs
in a bucket, all
scrambling around
for space, and instead
recognize that there's
room for us all to be
beautiful in our own
unique ways.

8

We Need to Talk About . . . Social Media

It looks like your average Instagram reel, something you might scroll past and not think too deeply about – a woman with glossy dark hair, in a grey sweatshirt, is waiting for her boyfriend to get home from golf. He told her he'd be home at a certain time, but a few hours pass and he's still not back. A TikTok user used this reel as an example to display how what we see on social media isn't always an accurate reflection of reality – when she opened the comments, most were full of users sending red flag emojis and saying that the girl's boyfriend was disrespecting her time. This reflected her own views too. But when the TikTok user sent the video to her boyfriend and told him to check the comments, the comments he was served were completely different – even though he viewed it at almost the exact same time as her.

He saw a bunch of comments that were completely on the golfer's side, telling the girl to get her own hobbies instead of waiting around for him.[57]

We learned about algorithms in Chapter 1. And while many of us are aware of how the content we see is based on what we've liked in the past, not many people realize that this extends even to people's comments on the content!

I don't know about you, but I often will look at the comment section to gain an understanding of how others are responding to posts and videos. I've always thought it's a helpful way of getting a grasp of different viewpoints. But if the algorithm is making us believe that everyone is responding to something in one particular way based on what it thinks we will agree with, our entire perspective on things is being manipulated!

Social media platforms haven't been around for that long. Instagram was first launched in 2010, and TikTok was first released in 2016. Yet the impact they have had on us is enormous. In earlier chapters, we discussed how to use social media to both educate ourselves and have impactful conversations. In this chapter, I want us to dig deeper into the impact social media has on how we as individuals function within society, how it influences our views; and whether it is stopping us from having the conversations we need to be having.

It's time we talked about social media.

Under the influence

Social media has become a form of social currency. We have moved into a space where we are led to believe that the number of followers or likes someone receives tells us something about them as a person. This can leave us hinging our self-esteem on something incredibly false and fleeting. Studies have shown that social media . . .

- **Elicits emotional distress.** One study showed that getting fewer 'likes' than others on a post can trigger emotional distress in adolescents.[58]
- **Makes us self-conscious and sad.** Academics from Oxford University, who are carrying out one of the largest global studies of teenage mental health, said that their initial research had found a linear relationship between higher rates of anxiety and depression and time spent on socal media sites.[59]
- **Takes up so much of our time.** According to one survey, the average American spends five hours and 16 minutes on their phone every day. That's the equivalent of a day and a half per week, and across the year that's around 80 days.[60]

But there are many benefits to social media. From connecting with others, giving the voiceless a voice and breaking down barriers, it can be used for lots of good things too. It . . .

- **Brings us friendship.** We can find people online with similar interests to us, connecting us to communities that we might not meet in real life. Studies have shown that social media may support the well-being of LGBTQIA+ youth as it enables peer connection.[61]

- **Helps us to be creative.** Artists, writers, make-up artists and photographers have been able to use social media as a virtual gallery and a place to share their work for free. In one study of US teenagers, 71 per cent said they loved how social media helped them show their creative side.[62]
- **Shows us different kinds of beauty.** If you follow a diverse group of people who celebrate the way they look and feel, it can encourage you to celebrate your own differences. A 2021 study in the US examined the impact of body-positive social media posts and found that they helped improve viewers' body image.[63]

We want these positive experiences of being on social media to outnumber the negatives. But I worry that they never will. Why? Because as much as we think we have control over our social media usage, we don't. I always say that we are renting space in a billionaire's backyard. These platforms are owned by incredibly rich people, and ultimately, how they function will always be in a way that serves those who make money from them rather than us, the users. This is why they are designed to be addictive. So, we stay on them and continue making more money for the platform owners.

Asking for these platforms to become more ethical therefore feels impossible. So, the best thing you can do is to be aware of the ways in which they are functioning. From there you can figure out how you want to use them in the way that best serves you. It's a way to hack the system.

I left Twitter when it became an unsafe place for me to be. I was receiving regular violent trolling, and the platform was doing little to make it safer for me and those like me. It's now owned by Elon Musk, who has renamed it X. He's the billionaire owner of the car company Tesla and is becoming increasingly far-right and offensive in his views – from transphobic comments to openly supporting gun rights and endorsing Donald Trump for president of the United States.[64] He wants his platform to echo his views and support them.

This means the content we see is not telling us the full picture. Ultimately, it's the company who decides whether or not anyone – even our own followers – sees our content. And many people with big followings are seeing that if you don't post opinions that reinforce the political values of the people who own the platform then those follower numbers mean nothing at all. It's all an illusion.

It's interesting and disappointing to consider that social media companies can intervene with our accounts and the content that we're shown in this way, but yet aren't interested in investing in software that would eradicate and target harassment, extremism, racism, misogyny and the other forms of abuse that happen on these platforms. They could be investing in making platforms more ethical, but they aren't.

Being aware of this can help us find a healthier balance. We can use our knowledge to have discussions, both with ourselves and others, as to how to best use social media in a way that serves *us*, not them. If we're aware that it's designed to be addictive, how can we use that knowledge to consider our own use of it? Do we build in breaks, such as not going on it at weekends or until the evenings?

Everyone has such a different relationship to social media, and what works for one person may not for another. But it's worth trying some different methods out and seeing if changing your usage improves your happiness and self-esteem.

Take TikTok. I know lots of people find it very fun, but I don't like to use it. After some time on it, I realized that the algorithm pushed me to go down wormholes that weren't in my best interests, and I was exposed to a lot of videos that could have been incredibly damaging to me. I first went on the platform looking for people who had similar mental health challenges to me, as I thought they could offer me ways to deal with my anxiety and PTSD and understand how I was feeling. But then I ended up on pages of people who were very severely mentally ill, and it was incredibly hard to bear witness to that suffering. I recognized that the only way for me to truly have a healthy relationship with the platform was to completely disengage. But it's up to you to figure out what's best for you and your mental health.

Take time to consider what you like about social media and what you hate about it. When you spend time on it, what's your overwhelming feeling? When you put your phone down, how do you feel about yourself? Think about the algorithm too – is it impacting your view on the world, and are there better places you could be going to for content – places that give you a fuller, more complete picture of the way things are? Use this to inform how you want to use it.

Are you trapped in an echo chamber?

If everywhere you look you see your own opinion echoed back to you, it's more than likely that you're in what's called an echo chamber. This is where you believe that the majority of people think like you do because that's all you ever see when you open your phone. But as we've been discussing, you're really at the mercy of algorithms, and there are a plethora of different views and perspectives out there that you're probably not seeing.

Ending up in an echo chamber is easily done – after all, it's natural to want to surround ourselves with like-minded people. There's comfort to be found in echo chambers, and I've found that they can so easily be confused with community. But the pitfall of an echo chamber is that you end up with the perception that everybody believes what you believe, as you're not paying attention to other perspectives.

Say you look across your social media and see that the majority of your friends have the same political stance as you. That's stopping you from seeing the full picture – from being able to recognize what's really going on in the world and what needs to be done to create change.

That's why it's so important to make sure that you're getting your news from more than one source, one paper or one website. Otherwise, you'll end up getting a very one-sided view of things. When you break out of your echo chamber, you may be confronted with things that you really don't agree with, but whether you agree with them or not, it's good to know those views exist in order to have the best conversations.

Echo chambers don't just hide the views of people we disagree with – they could also keep the experiences of other marginalized people away from us. By spending time with those similar to us or having our own views pushed back to us in our feeds, we may be missing vital voices that could help us with our cause.

Understanding the experiences of other people doesn't just help us to coexist, but to *resist* together as well across communities.

We as activists and people who want to work together to create change need to actively break out of our echo chambers. We need to find one another, understand each other's causes and how they're linked, and then fight back together.

Cancel culture

'I've been cancelled!' This is what high-profile people say when they have been held to account for saying or doing something that has caused harm or offence. Sometimes they're simply 'cancelled' by other people talking about what they did on social media, while in some cases they may lose work and have contracts withdrawn with the companies they work for.

A frustrating thing when you hear celebrities complain about being cancelled is that so often they're doing so across a six-page spread in a newspaper or to their thousands of followers. We see them talk about being 'silenced' while doing an interview on national television. Or even if they are facing some serious career repercussions, we tend to see many so-called 'cancelled' celebrities return to the public eye after a short period away.

High-profile people often blame 'cancel culture' for restricting their freedom of speech and silencing them. But that to me is just someone powerful throwing their toys out of the pram because they can't say or do harmful things any more without being held to account.

Before social media, when powerful people did harmful things, it was a lot harder to speak out against them. Of course, many activists staged protests, spoke to the media and fought to create change, but many didn't have the resources to get their message out far and wide. Now, this can be done on a scale like never before.

Look at . . .

- **the global #MeToo movement.** Launched by activist Tarana Burke, this movement gave people the courage to share their own stories of sexual harassment. It exposed high-profile sexual predators, such as the director Harvey Weinstein, who was subsequently convicted as a sex offender. The hashtag #MeToo was posted 19 million times in one year and led to the establishment of a legal defence fund with the aim to help those with less power and money be able to take workplace harassment cases to court.[65]

- **Stop Funding Hate:** This is a UK grassroots organization that encourages brands to stop advertising in newspapers that publish racist and anti-migrant content. As a result of this pressure, brands have pulled out of supporting certain newspapers, such as LEGO ending their promotional activity with the *Daily Mail*.

We are living in a time when marginalized communities are able to express disgust and anger at the way in which patriarchy, white supremacy, xenophobia, transphobia and homophobia operate within our society. We can challenge the corporations and people that profit from this and use our collective voice to start conversations about how wrong so many of these structures are. We've seen how this can bring about real change.

Yet those who don't like this, who want to uphold these old systems, try to gaslight us by calling this 'cancel culture'. Cancel culture is the collective boycotting of someone or something after an accusation of a socially unacceptable action. It is often criticized by people in positions of power who do not want to be challenged on their harmful behaviour and argue it prevents free speech.

They are wrong. It is resistance.

The truth is that the people in positions of power are the ones doing the silencing, stifling the voices of those who do not have the same platform or access to resources. It's powerful governments targeting refugees and restricting the healthcare of trans people. It's restrictions being put in place to limit our right to protest. They are trying to silence us, yet when we hold people to account for this, we're told we're 'cancelling' them, or restricting *their* right to free speech.

It's vital we do not let these false ideas about 'cancel culture' silence us. We have to keep having conversations. We need to keep talking.

Part 4

———

Turning Your Conversations into Actions

———

You and your voice have so much power – think of all the things we've discussed so far. Even just one conversation can create a ripple effect that continues to create more positive conversations and more change.

Every conversation and every cause is different, and there's no one-size-fits-all approach to what will bring about change.

Change could look like a productive, kind conversation with someone that gently shows them that their views could be harming others.

Or change could come about from bringing different communities together and finding ways to challenge the oppression that comes from the top.

Or change could come from you finding your cause, researching it, talking about it and spreading the word.

From there you can start to look at small actions that you could bring into your everyday life. I'm constantly looking for what I can do – whether it's big or small – to keep pushing my cause forward. As I said earlier, activism is active and so is allyship. Some of the most effective actions I have found are . . .

Boycotting. Money = power, and those who have it will do everything they can to ensure they keep it. This means ensuring that their businesses remain profitable and that we, as consumers, keep spending our money. We can use the power of our cash and where we spend it to influence businesses to operate in a more ethical way. We don't have as much money as the billionaires individually, but when we boycott as part of a movement, we are withdrawing our money *en* *masse* in such a powerful way that companies *have* to take notice.

We've seen, throughout history, how powerful boycotts can be. It was one of the elements that ended apartheid in South Africa. The Anti-Apartheid Movement encouraged people who opposed apartheid and the treatment of non-white people in South Africa to stop buying goods from businesses in the country that benefitted from it. For nearly 30 years the movement regularly updated its list of South African brand names to avoid, and while there were many other factors that led to the falling of apartheid, one of them is the fact that eventually it became financially unviable for South Africa to hold up that system of oppression.[66]

Contacting those in power. Before social media and rolling news channels, there was an element of the general public feeling far removed from those in power. But in recent years and in many countries across the world, there has been a move to make politics more easily digestible and accessible. Conversation channels have opened up so we can contact those who have the power to let them know what we think about the policies currently in place.

I'm based in the UK and whenever there's a debate going on or a law change being discussed, I will write to my MP either expressing how I'd like them to vote on a specific issue or to let them know how let down I feel by the decisions made by Parliament. Whether or not you see eye to eye with them, you always have to let your representatives know how you feel. If they don't respond after two weeks, keep following up with them. Or if they do local surgeries (meetings with the public), go and visit them and voice your concerns to them directly. These are people who were elected and are paid to represent you and your area's views. They have a responsibility to respond and engage with you, so keep pushing, even if you don't hear back.

Going along to a protest. Take your voice to the streets. It can be hard to speak out as an individual – you may feel like you don't know enough to engage in a one-on-one conversation about a topic, or that these discussions will be a drain on your energy. I feel that way often, and when I do, there's something so powerful about just taking my feet to the pavement and being part of a collective, visible voice for change.

Allies to a community should come along and join marches and protests too. I'm always encouraging cisgender people to come along to London Trans Pride, or to join their local Pride march. The more we show that it's not just our community who's opposed to transphobia, but the majority of people, the more likely those in power are to change their policies. Protests show those in power that their actions are not supported by a huge number of people and losing that support could impact how long they stay in power. It's about rallying the troops to challenge and show them that they may be in power now, but that doesn't mean they *always* will be.

Information about protests will be shared on online groups via social media or on the websites of the charities that support your cause. You don't have to go along to protests with friends, particularly as protests are a great way to meet like-minded people within your community, but it is vital that you pay attention to safety advice before going. Always let someone know where you are; wear comfortable, plain clothing; bring along water and snacks; and read up on your rights (which will differ depending on where your protest is) before you go. Once there, absorb as much as possible – really breathe in the sights and sounds surrounding you. You're in a crowd full of people who are angered and upset by the same thing as you, but who care enough to take action that will bring about change. That's powerful, and the memories of this will boost you, even on the most draining of days.

A final talking point from me . . .

We need to be observers of history, move with it and learn constantly. And remember – all of these actions come from the simple power of someone saying in a conversation, 'Shall we try . . .'

Conversations change the world – in huge, noticeable, system-shattering ways, but also in smaller, quieter and more subtle ones.

You might not think that your words will have any impact on the world, but there really is no greater act of defiance than using your voice.

Resources

Mental health services
Campaign Against Living Miserably
www.thecalmzone.net
Family Lives
www.familylives.org.uk
Mind
www.mind.org.uk
YoungMinds
www.youngminds.org.uk

Wellbeing services
Anti-Bullying Alliance
www.anti-bullyingalliance.org.uk
Beat
www.beateatingdisorders.org.uk
Childline
www.childline.org.uk
National Bullying Helpline
www.nationalbullyinghelpline.co.uk
Shout
www.giveusashout.org

LGBTQIA+ services

Albert Kennedy Trust
www.akt.org.uk
LGBT Foundation
www. lgbt.foundation
LGBT Switchboard
www.switchboard.lgbt
MindOut
www.mindout.org.uk
Terrence Higgins Trust
www.tht.org.uk
The Proud Trust
www.theproudtrust.org

Gender identity services

Gendered Intelligence
www.genderedintelligence.co.uk
Mermaids
www.mermaidsuk.org.uk

Housing services

Centrepoint
www.centrepoint.org.uk
Shelter
www.shelter.org.uk

Domestic violence services

Galop
www.galop.org.uk

Refuge
www.refuge.org.uk
Respect
www.respect.org.uk
www.mensadviceline.org.uk
SafeLives
www.safelives.org.uk
Women's Aid
www.womensaid.org.uk

Sexual abuse services
Safeline
www.safeline.org.uk
SARSAS
www.sarsas.org.uk
The Survivor's Trust
www.thesurvivorstrust.org

Substance abuse services
Frank
www.talktofrank.com
Via
www.viaorg.uk

Further reading
Amelia Abraham, *Queer Intentions: A (Personal) Journey Through LGBTQ+ Culture*
Akala, *Natives: Race and Class in the Ruins of Empire*
Travis Alabanza, *None of the Above: Reflections on Life Beyond the Binary*

Margaret Atwood, *The Handmaid's Tale*

Aja Barber, *Consumed: The Need for Collective Change; Colonialism, Climate Change & Consumerism*

Charlie Brinkhurst-Cuff and Timi Sotire, *Black Joy: A Collection of Love Letters to Black British Culture*

Judith Butler, *Who's Afraid of Gender?*

Scarlett Curtis, *Feminists Don't Wear Pink (and Other Lies)*

Emma Dabiri, *Disobedient Bodies: Reclaim Your Unruly Beauty*

Emma Dabiri, *Twisted: The Tangled History of Black Hair Culture*

Juno Dawson, *What's the T? The No-nonsense Guide to All Things Trans and/or Non-binary for Teens*

Reni Eddo-Lodge, *Why I'm No Longer Talking to White People About Race*

Shon Faye, *The Transgender Issue*

Gigi Gorgeous and Gottmik with Swan Huntley, *The T Guide: Our Trans Experiences and a Celebration of Gender Expression – Man, Woman, Nonbinary and Beyond*

Afua Hirsch, *Brit(ish): On Race, Identity and Belonging*

bell hooks, *All About Love: New Visions*

bell hooks, *The Will to Change: Men, Masculinity, and Love*

Tiffany Jewell, *This Book is Anti-Racist: 20 Lessons on How to Wake Up, Take Action, and Do the Work*

Mariam Khan, *It's Not About the Burqa: Muslim Women on Faith, Feminism, Sexuality and Race*

Naomi Klein, *Doppelganger: A Trip into the Mirror World*

Cariad Lloyd, *You Are Not Alone: A New Way to Grieve*

Gina Martin, *Be The Change: A Toolkit for the Activist in You*

Janet Mock, *Redefining Realness: My Path to Womanhood, Identity, Love & So Much More*

Elliot Page, *Pageboy: A Memoir*

Zing Tsjeng, The Forgotten Women series

Raquel Willis, *The Risk It Takes to Bloom: On Life and Liberation*

Acknowledgements

Thinking back on my journey into activism, which began
over a decade ago . . . I would never have thought that
all of those experiences, the highs and lows, the setbacks,
lessons and achievements, would culminate in a book to
help others find their voice, understand their own capacity
to bring about change and most importantly, to talk to
each other and find a common ground.

The world today feels very different to when I first
started campaigning for transgender rights and racial
equality. We've seen so much change, both progress and
pushback, elation and devastation, but if I've learned
anything during that time, it's that the pendulum rarely
swings in a linear fashion. There's a power in embracing
the unpredictability of change, in recognizing the fragility
of our rights and understanding activism as a constant
practice of protecting and preserving the best parts of what
it means to be human.

I want to take this moment to thank all of my mentors
who have encouraged, supported and inspired me over the
past ten years. Thank you for your patience, for nurturing
the spark and teaching me to see my hope for the world
as an active responsibility that I have to myself and to

others. I wouldn't be able to pass on these lessons to a new generation without a lifetime of guidance from my trans and queer elders. *Talk To Me* truly stands on the shoulders of giants. I hope it makes you proud.

Many thanks to my phenomenal editors, Phoebe Jascourt and India Chambers, for your support throughout this process, and thank you to the entire team at Penguin Random House for trusting me to write this book. Thank you for valuing my insights and giving me the opportunity to share what I have learned with the world. We have found ourselves in an increasingly complicated moment in history, and I hope *Talk To Me* finds its way into the hands of those in need of the same invaluable guidance that I have been fortunate enough to receive over the years.

Thank you to Abigail Bergstrom at Bergstrom Studio, the most incredible literary agent I could dream of. Your passion for supporting emerging authors who want to see the world change for the better is incredible. Thank you for pushing me to create the best work possible, for constantly challenging me as an author and bringing me back to centre when the inevitable mid-project spiral hits. *Talk To Me* wouldn't have been possible without your guidance and encouragement over the past seven years of us working together.

Finally, thank you to you, the reader. If this book has found its way into your hands or ears, I hope it serves you well. I hope it acts as a springboard of self-realization and motivates you to see the opportunity in every adversity. Our ability to see the humanity in each other, to speak to each other with respect and patience, to afford each other the dignity we all deserve as human beings, is crucial if we want to see a sustained progress that is inclusive of us all. I hope *Talk To Me* helps those difficult conversations feel a little less daunting and, one exchange at a time, helps to close the perceived distance that is pushing us apart. Thank you for going on this journey with me, and I wish you the best as you continue on yours.

Index

Sources

1 https://www.theguardian.com/world/2024/feb/02/
  first-edition-gen-z-men-women-political
2 https://www.un.org/en/climatechange/science/
  causes-effects-climate-change
3 https://www.ofcom.org.uk/__data/assets/pdf_
  file/0024/264651/news-consumption-2023.pdf
4 https://www.rollingstone.com/pro/features/
  music-business-blackout-tuesday-1008685/
5 https://www.bbc.co.uk/news/
  uk-england-london-56594570
6 https://www.theguardian.com/education/2018/sep/12/
  london-school-that-told-boy-to-cut-off-dreadlocks-backs-
  down
7 https://www.standard.co.uk/lifestyle/london-life/
  munroe-bergdorf-people-wouldn-t-go-over-to-someone-
  s-mother-and-ask-about-their-labia-but-they-re-happy-to-
  come-over-to-a-trans-person-and-ask-about-their-genitals-
  9491573.html
8 https://qz.com/quartzy/1597688/a-brief-history-of-
  women-in-pants
9 https://www.parliament.uk/about/living-heritage/
  transformingsociety/private-lives/relationships/overview/
  sexuality20thcentury/
10 https://en.wikipedia.org/wiki/Jim_Crow_laws
11 https://www.bbc.co.uk/bbcthree/article/cacc0b40-c3a4-
   473b-86cc-11863c0b3f30

12 https://www.margaretthatcher.org/document/106941
13 https://www.bbc.co.uk/news/articles/c4nng2j42xro
   https://www.telegraph.co.uk/politics/2024/07/01/labour-
   frontbencher-refuses-to-answer-trans-toilet-question/
14 https://www.bbc.com/news/education-69017920
15 https://www.vox.com/identities/2020/6/23/21295432/
   police-black-trans-people-violence
   https://www.met.police.uk/foi-ai/metropolitan-
   police/disclosure-2023/november-2023/
   officers-placed-under-investigation-homophobic-
   transphobic-behaviour-2018-2023/
   https://www.bbc.co.uk/news/articles/c044405zd7ko
   https://www.thestar.co.uk/news/gross-misconduct-proven-
   for-officer-who-had-transphobic-and-racist-memes-on-
   phone-4695964
16 https://www.thepinknews.com/2024/06/27/rishi-sunak-
   keir-starmer-trans-rights/
   https://www.dazeddigital.com/life-culture/article/62944/1/
   keir-starmer-gender-ideology-being-taught-in-schools-
   pride-right-wing
   https://www.thetimes.com/uk/politics/article/keir-starmer-
   labour-general-election-interview-m7m787cd2
17 https://www.theguardian.com/society/2023/oct/03/
   trans-hospital-patients-in-england-to-be-banned-from-
   female--and-male-only-wards
18 https://www.theguardian.com/uk-news/2023/mar/21/
   metropolitan-police-institutionally-racist-misogynistic-
   homophobic-louise-casey-report
19 https://galop.org.uk/wp-content/uploads/2021/06/Trans-
   Hate-Crime-Report-2020.pdf
20 https://williamsinstitute.law.ucla.edu/press/ncvs-trans-
   press-release/
21 https://www.bbc.co.uk/news/newsbeat-55249400
   https://www.hrmagazine.co.uk/content/news/
   afro-hair-styles-still-considered-unprofessional-study-finds/
22 https://gcn.ie/trans-activists-protest-nhs-england/

23 https://www.dazeddigital.com/life-culture/article/65702/1/
young-trans-activists-trans-kids-deserve-better-wes-
streeting-office
https://www.stonewall.org.uk/news/
stonewall-responds-to-indefinite-puberty-blockers-ban-
announced-by-government

24 https://www.met.police.uk/SysSiteAssets/foi-media/
metropolitan-police/disclosure_2022/june_2022/
policies-gender-reassignment-transgender-non-binary-
officers-staff-volunteers-qas.docx

25 https://www.theguardian.com/society/2023/oct/05/
record-rise-hate-crimes-transgender-people-reported-
england-and-wales

26 https://www.theguardian.com/us-news/2022/dec/16/
us-trans-non-binary-youth-suicide-mental-health

27 https://www.ethnicity-facts-figures.service.gov.uk/
crime-justice-and-the-law/policing/number-of-arrests/
latest/#main-facts-and-figures
https://prisonreformtrust.org.uk/project/race/

28 https://www.pewtrusts.org/en/research-and-analysis/
issue-briefs/2023/05/racial-disparities-persist-in-many-us-
jails

29 https://www.theguardian.com/austaustralia-news/2020/
jul/16/nts-indigenous-young-people-43-times-more-likely-
to-go-to-jail-than-non-indigenous-youth

30 https://www.investopedia.com/articles/investing/062215/
business-model-private-prisons.asp

31 https://news.npcc.police.uk/releases/
police-action-plan-launched-aiming-to-address-race-
disparities-affecting-black-people-and-change-a-legacy-of
distrust

32 https://www.pewresearch.org/short-reads/2020/06/03/
10-things-we-know-about-race-and-policing-in-the-u-s/

33 https://www.theguardian.com/australia-news/2023/jul/31/
nsw-police-use-force-against-indigenous-australians-at-
drastically-disproportionate-levels-data-shows

34 https://www.theguardian.com/uk-news/2024/feb/02/
brianna-ghey-murderers-named-sentenced-to-life-in-prison

35 https://edition.cnn.com/2021/10/09/uk/uk-trans-rights-
gender-critical-media-intl-gbr-cmd/index.html

36 https://www.reuters.com/world/us/trump-expected-
highlight-murder-michigan-woman-immigration-speech-
2024-04-02/

37 https://www.pressreader.com/uk/daily-mail/20150731/page/1
https://www.express.co.uk/news/politics/658502/Record-
illegal-migrants-entered-EU-ONE-year-Brexit

38 https://www.theguardian.com/uk-news/article/2024/jul/24/
shoplifting-rate-england-wales-rises-new-20-year-high

39 https://www.bbc.co.uk/news/entertainment-arts-63469444

40 https://www.forbes.com/sites/evaepker/2023/10/31/
women-handle-75-of-all-unpaid-labor-their-health-pays-
the-price/

41 https://www.statista.com/topics/2229/billionaires-around-
the-world/

42 https://www.independent.co.uk/news/marriage-live-
longer-bachelors-heart-study-b2288786.html
https://ifstudies.org/blog/who-is-happiest-married-
mothers-and-fathers-per-the-latest-general-social-survey
https://www.cnbc.com/2018/09/21/married-men-are-
earning-much-more-money-than-everyone-else-in-
america.html
https://journals.sagepub.com/doi/10.1177/
19485506241287960

43 https://www.bbc.co.uk/news/education-68731795

44 https://www.theguardian.com/news/2024/feb/01/
gen-z-boys-and-men-more-likely-than-baby-boomers-to-
believe-feminism-harmful-says-poll

45 https://www.personneltoday.com/hr/green-park-business-
leaders-index-2021-ftse-100-diversity-inclusion/

46 https://journals.plos.org/plosone/article?id=10.1371/
journal.pone.0212852

47 https://www.nytimes.com/2024/02/28/books/publishing-books-poc-dei.html

48 https://www.npr.org/2024/04/11/1243713272/resume-bias-study-white-names-black-names

49 https://www.cnbc.com/2023/10/19/nearly-20percent-of-job-candidates-have-changed-their-names-on-resumes-because-of-discrimination-concerns.html

50 https://www.hrmagazine.co.uk/content/comment/it-s-not-just-hair-hair-discrimination-in-the-workplace/

51 https://www.stonewall.org.uk/resources/lgbt-britain-work-report-2018

52 https://www.theguardian.com/world/2018/apr/23/skin-lightening-creams-are-dangerous-yet-business-is-booming-can-the-trade-be-stopped

53 https://www.dailymail.co.uk/tvshowbiz/article-10433771/Kim-Kardashian-famous-family-amassed-1-2BILLION-Instagram-followers.html

54 https://www.thesun.co.uk/tvandshowbiz/28681395/kourtney-kardashian-claps-back-weight-baby-rocky/

55 https://www.cosmopolitan.com/uk/body/health/a37958983/khloe-kardashian-stopped-fad-diets/

56 https://people.com/tv/kim-kardashian-west-why-she-tried-to-hide-her-body-after-saint-wests-birth/

57 https://www.reddit.com/r/interestingasfuck/comments/1d19zo6/apparently_different_comments_show_up_on_videos/?rdt=54278

58 https://www.ncbi.nlm.nih.gov/pmc/articles/PMC7722198/

59 https://www.ft.com/content/bced2138-366b-448f-ab12-3c068199145a

60 https://www.harmonyhit.com/phone-screen-time-statistics/

61 https://www.ncbi.nlm.nih.gov/books/

62 https://www.pewresearch.org/internet/2022/11/16/connection-creativity-and-drama-teen-life-on-social-media-in-2022/

63 https://www.healthline.com/health/social-media-and-body-image

64 https://www.washingtonpost.com/business/2024/07/26/musk-transgender-vivian-grimes/
https://www.independent.co.uk/news/elon-musk-twitter-transgender-hate-speech-b2351923.html
https://www.nbcnews.com/tech/tech-news/elon-musk-raises-payment-offer-100-voters-sign-petition-rcna176075
https://www.foxnews.com/politics/elon-musk-minces-no-words-pledging-support-second-amendment-tyrants-disarm-people

65 https://thesocialchangeagency.org/blog/times-up-the-next-iteration-of-the-metoo-movement/

66 https://www.theguardian.com/world/2021/may/23/israel-apartheid-boycotts-sanctions-south-africa